Remember the Poor

How the Earliest Christians Cared for the Needy

A Tool for Making the Case for Mercy in Your Congregation

D1607977

An in-depth study with questions for group use

by Matthew C. Harrison

CONCORDIA PUBLISHING HOUSE · SAINT LOUIS

Published by Concordia Publishing House
3558 S. Jefferson Ave., St. Louis, MO 63118-3968
1-800-325-3040 • www.cph.org

Copyright © 2018 The Lutheran Church—Missouri Synod

Library of Congress Cataloging-in-Publication Data

Names: Harrison, Matthew C., author.

Title: Remember the poor : How the earliest Christians cared for the needy; a tool for making the case for mercy in your congregation / by Matthew C. Harrison.

Description: Saint Louis : Concordia Publishing House, 2018. | Includes bibliographical references and index. |

Identifiers: LCCN 2017058269 (print) | LCCN 2018004026 (ebook) | ISBN 9780758661067 | ISBN 9780758661029 (alk. paper)

Subjects: LCSH: Bible. New Testament--Criticism, interpretation, etc. | Church fund raising--Biblical teaching. | Mercy--Biblical teaching.

Classification: LCC BS2545.C554 (ebook) | LCC BS2545.C554 H37 2018 (print) | DDC 225.6/7--dc23

LC record available at https://lccn.loc.gov/2017058269

Manufactured in the United States of America

1   2   3   4   5   6   7   8   9   10   27   26   25   24   23   22   21   20   19   18

Contents

Preface

One of the constant callings and simultaneous challenges for the church is to embody Christ's presence in concrete acts of charity and mercy. As the faithful hear the living voice of Jesus through His apostles and prophets, and as they experience His presence at the font and the altar, they are to live out this gracious reality of God's mercy and compassion in Christ. Matthew C. Harrison's study of Paul's collection for Jerusalem displays how Paul's theology was embodied in this apostolic effort. The examination of scriptural texts is scholarly and thorough. At the same time, the author goes beyond exegetical research that remains abstract. Rather, Harrison persuasively recommends that Paul's practice is the appropriate paradigm for churchly care and compassion for the neighbor in the twenty-first century. Here is a refreshing, scriptural antidote to a sterile and abstract orthodoxy on the one hand, and liberalism's empty effort to do good on the other hand. Here, Christ and His gifts permeate the actions as well as the thought of the church. Readers will benefit from this insightful exposition of a frequently neglected aspect of Paul's apostolic mission.

May the church hear afresh Paul's invitation: "Be imitators of me, as I am of Christ" (1 Corinthians 11:1).

Dean O. Wenthe
SEPTEMBER 2007

Foreword

In 2007, I was able to find a little time to work on the topic of St. Paul's great collection for Jerusalem. There is so very much packed into this issue in the New Testament, and as I hope the reader will see, so much of the vital heartbeat of Paul's theology resonates for him in this issue, which one scholar has called Paul's "obsession." The issues of grace, fellowship, mercy, mission, and others all coincide at the point of the collection. Even more, tracing the history of the collection through the New Testament documents gives enlightenment on the whole sociocultural reality faced by the New Testament church.

You will see that for St. Paul, demonstrating mercy as a corporate churchly act was serious business that took up much of his Christian life. It was deeply intertwined with his view of the Gospel and of the church's mission. Finally, it was delivering the gifts to Jerusalem that led to his imprisonment and ultimate martyrdom.

This paper was written for a PhD course at Concordia Seminary, St. Louis, for Dr. Jeffrey Oschwald, a delightful, humble expert on the New Testament who added much and forced the answering of numerous questions. This study is but a beginning. It is about the "nuts and bolts" and dates of the collection and its place in the New Testament.

As I am a "church bureaucrat" who finds himself ill at ease with life strictly governed by policy, budgets, bylaws, and generally accepted accounting principles (all a necessity in this fallen world), drinking deep of the New Testament on this issue was a breath of fresh air. But it was also delightful to find that Paul's dealing with the collection was "big business" for the earliest church, and 2 Corinthians (as Betz demonstrates handily in his commentary) shows that Paul was operating in this matter with the clear language and principles of the legal and business world of his day. There is a practical, left-hand kingdom side to working together as a fellowship of faith, as church.

Knowing something of the great collection is vital for anyone who actually desires to get something real done in the church on behalf of Christ. From fund development to personnel, to government regulations and internal power struggles, St. Paul dealt with it all. And by God's grace, he found a way to assist the needy in all of it. That's comforting and encouraging. Where the mercy of Christ in the Gospel provides the heartbeat, there is a way to get it done. "Let's go" (Mark 1:38).

Matthew C. Harrison
ST. LOUIS, MO, 2008

Map of Paul's Missionary Journeys

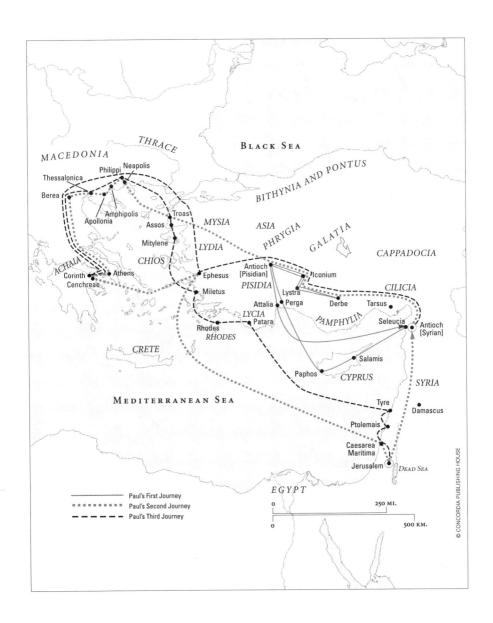

MACEDONIA
THRACE
BLACK SEA
BITHYNIA AND PONTUS
Thessalonica
Philippi
Neapolis
Berea
Amphipolis
Apollonia
Assos
Troas
MYSIA
ASIA
PHRYGIA
GALATIA
CAPPADOCIA
Mitylene
LYDIA
CHIOS
ACHAIA
Corinth
Athens
Ephesus
Antioch [Pisidian]
Iconium
CILICIA
Cenchreae
Miletus
PISIDIA
Lystra
Attalia
Perga
Derbe
Tarsus
LYCIA
Patara
PAMPHYLIA
Seleucia
Antioch [Syrian]
Rhodes
RHODES
CRETE
Salamis
Paphos
CYPRUS
SYRIA
MEDITERRANEAN SEA
Tyre
Damascus
Ptolemais
Caesarea Maritima
Jerusalem
DEAD SEA
EGYPT

Paul's First Journey
Paul's Second Journey
Paul's Third Journey

0   250 MI.
0   500 KM.

© CONCORDIA PUBLISHING HOUSE

Paul's Collection for Jerusalem

INTRODUCTION

The church can learn a great deal from studying Paul's great collection for Jerusalem. While the famous "stewardship" texts of 2 Corinthians 8 and 9 are regularly recited in efforts to raise funds for operations or special projects in the church's life and mission, or in stewardship education materials, they are more rarely referenced in specific relation to the context that elicited them from the apostle. The fundamental context and reason for the chief apostolic teaching on the sharing of one's possessions, and those of the church as a corporate entity (particularly money), is the alleviation of pressing need among fellow Christians. Overlooking the nature of the great collection also brings a neglect of several significant and even central Pauline themes in the New Testament. Numerous significant points of Paul's theology converge at the collection. Second Corinthians 8–9 alone brims with references to *charis* (grace), *koinonia* (participation/fellowship), *diakonia* (service, ministry), *spoudeis* (free, eager desire), *eulogia* (blessing), *ergon agathon* (good works), *eucharistia* (thanksgiving), *leitourgia* (public service), *genemata tes dikaiosunes* (harvest of righteousness), and others. These are the most powerful and freighted theological terms of the New Testament. Paul uses them all (and others) about or related to the collection for the poor. But more than anything else, this collection demonstrates the integration of Paul's pastoral heart, his theology, and his dedication to missions.[1]

At first glance, the apparent dearth of references to the collection in the Book of Acts presents somewhat of a conundrum. How important was the collection to St. Paul? How significant was it for his compatriots and, in general, for the churches he helped to found? Why might Luke in Acts limit references to the collection? The answers to these questions

---

1 See James Dunn, *The Theology of Paul the Apostle* (Grand Rapids: Eerdmans, 1998), 707.

will bear directly upon our assessment of the role of the church today in caring for the poor and needy in its midst. Since Acts is the great book of mission in the Early Church, only one or two clearly direct references in the book to the great collection would seem to relegate this aspect of the church's life to the periphery. Yet the evidence paints a different picture.

In Acts 24:17–18, there occurs the only overt and specific reference in the Book of Acts to Paul's great collection for the poor in Jerusalem. Jews caught up in the Zealot movement accosted Paul at the temple in AD 58. The Zealots were Jewish nationalists who worked to overthrow Roman rule and the influence of Greek culture during this time period.[2] The Jewish establishment accused Paul of false doctrine. Charges were proffered to Governor Felix. Paul stated in his defense: [17]*Now after several years I came to bring alms to my nation and to present offerings.* [18]*While I was doing this, they found me purified in the temple, without any crowd or tumult* (Acts 24:17–18). This incident soon began Paul's Caesarean house arrest of AD 59–60, during which time he likely wrote Philemon, Colossians, Ephesians, and 2 Timothy. The chain of events begun with the delivery of the "alms" "after several years" (Acts 24:17) of work soon took Paul to Rome and, finally, to martyrdom. The delivery of the alms was a decisive event for the beginning of the end of the apostle's earthly life. It was the culmination of an effort of considerable duration and complexity. The collection was intricately intertwined with Paul's mission and theology. Of all the ways Paul might have defended or defined his vocation in front of Caesar's representative, he chose to reference the collection. All this is veiled by this significant but undetailed and lone remark in Acts, which is part of Paul's speech to Felix.

How significant was the great collection for Paul? To answer this question, we must look at the time (when?), people (who?), places (where?), and rationale (what for?) involved in the greatest New Testament work of Christian charity. To this end, I shall provide a brief commentary on 2 Corinthians 8 and 9. In preparing what follows, I have made extensive use of three resources: (1) Bo Reicke, *Re-examining Paul's Letters: The History of the Pauline Correspondence* (2001); (2) Hans Dieter Betz, *2 Corinthians*

---

2 Bo Reicke, *Re-examining Paul's Letters: The History of the Pauline Correspondence* (Harrisburg, PA: Trinity Press International, 2001), 10.

8 and 9: A Commentary on Two Administrative Letters of the Apostle Paul (1985); and (3) Keith F. Nickle, *The Collection: A Study in Paul's Strategy* (1966). Reicke provides a thoroughgoing yet concise and readable explanation of all issues relative to the dating of the Pauline corpus. Reicke takes a refreshingly positive view of the veracity, authenticity, and integrity of the Pauline corpus, yet with deep scholarly fidelity. Reicke also paints an invaluable picture of the struggle of first-century Judaism against its Roman and Greek world and how the Christian movement fits into the mix. While both Betz and Nickle regularly question the historical accuracy of Acts and question the integrity of 2 Corinthians, both provide an overwhelming wealth of sources, resources, information, and studied expertise on all matters relating to the collection and the Pauline texts. This paper could not have been written without these three resources.

I have not engaged critical arguments regarding the integrity of the text or the historicity of the New Testament as these issues are raised by study of the collection. The purpose of this paper is simply to summarize, but in a reasonably complete fashion, the issue of Paul's great collection and what it meant for the first century. It is my conviction that the collection's significance does not lie merely in the first century, but that these texts and their meaning and history have much to say to the church today regarding the church's corporate diakonic life.

THE COLLECTION TEXTS

Acts 11
(Events Took Place AD 46)

11:19 Now those who were scattered because of the persecution that arose over Stephen traveled as far as Phoenicia and Cyprus and Antioch, speaking the word to no one except Jews. [20]But there were some of them, men of Cyprus and Cyrene, who on coming to Antioch spoke to the Hellenists also, preaching the Lord Jesus. [21]And the hand of the Lord was with them, and a great number who believed turned to the Lord. [22]The report of this came to the ears of the church in Jerusalem, and they sent Barnabas to Antioch. [23]When he came and saw the grace of God, he was glad, and he exhorted them all to remain faithful to the Lord with steadfast purpose, [24]for he was a good man, full of the Holy Spirit and of faith. And a great many people were added to the Lord. [25]So Barnabas went to Tarsus to look for Saul, [26]and when he had found him, he brought him to Antioch. For a whole year they met with the church and taught a great many people. And in Antioch the disciples were first called Christians.

[27]Now in these days prophets came down from Jerusalem to Antioch. [28]And one of them named Agabus stood up and foretold by the Spirit that there would be a great famine over all the world (this took place in the days of Claudius). [29]So the disciples determined, everyone according to his ability, to send relief to the brothers living in Judea. [30]And they did so, sending it to the elders by the hand of Barnabas and Saul.

Galatians 2
(Events Took Place AD 49)

2:1 Then after fourteen years I went up again to Jerusalem with Barnabas, taking Titus along with me. ²I went up because of a revelation and set before them (though privately before those who seemed influential) the gospel that I proclaim among the Gentiles, in order to make sure I was not running or had not run in vain. ³But even Titus, who was with me, was not forced to be circumcised, though he was a Greek. ⁴Yet because of false brothers secretly brought in—who slipped in to spy out our freedom that we have in Christ Jesus, so that they might bring us into slavery—⁵to them we did not yield in submission even for a moment, so that the truth of the gospel might be preserved for you. ⁶And from those who seemed to be influential (what they were makes no difference to me; God shows no partiality)—those, I say, who seemed influential added nothing to me. ⁷On the contrary, when they saw that I had been entrusted with the gospel to the uncircumcised, just as Peter had been entrusted with the gospel to the circumcised ⁸(for He who worked through Peter for his apostolic ministry to the circumcised worked also through me for mine to the Gentiles), ⁹and when James and Cephas and John, who seemed to be pillars, perceived the grace that was given to me, they gave the right hand of fellowship to Barnabas and me, that we should go to the Gentiles and they to the circumcised. ¹⁰Only, they asked us to remember the poor, the very thing I was eager to do.

1 Corinthians 16
(Spring AD 56)

16:1 Now concerning the collection for the saints: as I directed the churches of Galatia, so you also are to do. ²On the first day of every week, each of you is to put something aside and store it up, as he may prosper, so that there will be no collecting when I come. ³And when I arrive, I will send those whom you accredit by letter to carry your gift to Jerusalem. ⁴If it seems advisable that I should go also, they will accompany me.

⁵I will visit you after passing through Macedonia, for I intend to pass through Macedonia, ⁶and perhaps I will stay with you or even spend the

winter, so that you may help me on my journey, wherever I go. [7]For I do not want to see you now just in passing. I hope to spend some time with you, if the Lord permits. [8]But I will stay in Ephesus until Pentecost, [9]for a wide door for effective work has opened to me, and there are many adversaries.

[10]When Timothy comes, see that you put him at ease among you, for he is doing the work of the Lord, as I am. [11]So let no one despise him. Help him on his way in peace, that he may return to me, for I am expecting him with the brothers.

2 Corinthians 8 and 9
(Summer AD 57)

8:1 We want you to know, brothers, about the grace of God that has been given among the churches of Macedonia, [2]for in a severe test of affliction, their abundance of joy and their extreme poverty have overflowed in a wealth of generosity on their part. [3]For they gave according to their means, as I can testify, and beyond their means, of their own free will, [4]begging us earnestly for the favor of taking part in the relief of the saints—[5]and this, not as we expected, but they gave themselves first to the Lord and then by the will of God to us. [6]Accordingly, we urged Titus that as he had started, so he should complete among you this act of grace. [7]But as you excel in everything—in faith, in speech, in knowledge, in all earnestness, and in our love for you—see that you excel in this act of grace also.

[8]I say this not as a command, but to prove by the earnestness of others that your love also is genuine. [9]For you know the grace of our Lord Jesus Christ, that though He was rich, yet for your sake He became poor, so that you by His poverty might become rich. [10]And in this matter I give my judgment: this benefits you, who a year ago started not only to do this work but also to desire to do it. [11]So now finish doing it as well, so that your readiness in desiring it may be matched by your completing it out of what you have. [12]For if the readiness is there, it is acceptable according to what a person has, not according to what he does not have. [13]For I do not mean that others should be eased and you burdened, but that as a matter of fairness [14]your abundance at the present time should supply their need, so that their abundance may supply your need, that there may

be fairness. [15]As it is written, "Whoever gathered much had nothing left over, and whoever gathered little had no lack."

[16]But thanks be to God, who put into the heart of Titus the same earnest care I have for you. [17]For he not only accepted our appeal, but being himself very earnest he is going to you of his own accord. [18]With him we are sending the brother who is famous among all the churches for his preaching of the gospel. [19]And not only that, but he has been appointed by the churches to travel with us as we carry out this act of grace that is being ministered by us, for the glory of the Lord Himself and to show our good will. [20]We take this course so that no one should blame us about this generous gift that is being administered by us, [21]for we aim at what is honorable not only in the Lord's sight but also in the sight of man. [22]And with them we are sending our brother whom we have often tested and found earnest in many matters, but who is now more earnest than ever because of his great confidence in you. [23]As for Titus, he is my partner and fellow worker for your benefit. And as for our brothers, they are messengers of the churches, the glory of Christ. [24]So give proof before the churches of your love and of our boasting about you to these men.

9:1 Now it is superfluous for me to write to you about the ministry for the saints, [2]for I know your readiness, of which I boast about you to the people of Macedonia, saying that Achaia has been ready since last year. And your zeal has stirred up most of them. [3]But I am sending the brothers so that our boasting about you may not prove empty in this matter, so that you may be ready, as I said you would be. [4]Otherwise, if some Macedonians come with me and find that you are not ready, we would be humiliated—to say nothing of you—for being so confident. [5]So I thought it necessary to urge the brothers to go on ahead to you and arrange in advance for the gift you have promised, so that it may be ready as a willing gift, not as an exaction.

[6]The point is this: whoever sows sparingly will also reap sparingly, and whoever sows bountifully will also reap bountifully. [7]Each one must give as he has decided in his heart, not reluctantly or under compulsion, for God loves a cheerful giver. [8]And God is able to make all grace abound to you, so that having all sufficiency in all things at all times, you may abound in every good work. [9]As it is written,

"He has distributed freely, He has given to the poor;
His righteousness endures forever."

[10]He who supplies seed to the sower and bread for food will supply and multiply your seed for sowing and increase the harvest of your righteousness. [11]You will be enriched in every way to be generous in every way, which through us will produce thanksgiving to God. [12]For the ministry of this service is not only supplying the needs of the saints but is also overflowing in many thanksgivings to God. [13]By their approval of this service, they will glorify God because of your submission that comes from your confession of the gospel of Christ, and the generosity of your contribution for them and for all others, [14]while they long for you and pray for you, because of the surpassing grace of God upon you. [15]Thanks be to God for His inexpressible gift! [emphasis added]

Romans 15
(AD 58)

15:22 This is the reason why I have so often been hindered from coming to you. [23]But now, since I no longer have any room for work in these regions, and since I have longed for many years to come to you, [24]I hope to see you in passing as I go to Spain, and to be helped on my journey there by you, once I have enjoyed your company for a while. [25]At present, however, I am going to Jerusalem bringing aid to the saints. [26]For Macedonia and Achaia have been pleased to make some contribution for the poor among the saints at Jerusalem. [27]For they were pleased to do it, and indeed they owe it to them. For if the Gentiles have come to share in their spiritual blessings, they ought also to be of service to them in material blessings. [28]When therefore I have completed this and have delivered to them what has been collected, I will leave for Spain by way of you. [29]I know that when I come to you I will come in the fullness of the blessing of Christ.

[30]I appeal to you, brothers, by our Lord Jesus Christ and by the love of the Spirit, to strive together with me in your prayers to God on my behalf, [31]that I may be delivered from the unbelievers in Judea, and that my service for Jerusalem may be acceptable to the saints, [32]so that by

God's will I may come to you with joy and be refreshed in your company. [33]May the God of peace be with you all. Amen.

Acts 20
(Events Took Place AD 58)

20:1 After the uproar ceased, Paul sent for the disciples, and after encouraging them, he said farewell and departed for Macedonia. [2]When he had gone through those regions and had given them much encouragement, he came to Greece. [3]There he spent three months, and when a plot was made against him by the Jews as he was about to set sail for Syria, he decided to return through Macedonia. [4]Sopater of Berea, the son of Pyrrhus from Berea, accompanied him; and of the Thessalonians, Aristarchus and Secundus; and Gaius of Derbe, and Timothy; and the Asians, Tychicus and Trophimus. [5]These went on ahead and were waiting for us at Troas, [6]but we sailed away from Philippi after the days of Unleavened Bread, and in five days we came to them at Troas, where we stayed for seven days.

Acts 24
(Events Took Place AD 58–60)

24:10 And when the governor had nodded to him to speak, Paul replied: "Knowing that for many years you have been a judge over this nation, I cheerfully make my defense. [11]You can verify that it is not more than twelve days since I went up to worship in Jerusalem, [12]and they did not find me disputing with anyone or stirring up a crowd, either in the temple or in the synagogues or in the city. [13]Neither can they prove to you what they now bring up against me. [14]But this I confess to you, that according to the Way, which they call a sect, I worship the God of our fathers, believing everything laid down by the Law and written in the Prophets, [15]having a hope in God, which these men themselves accept, that there will be a resurrection of both the just and the unjust. [16]So I always take pains to have a clear conscience toward both God and man. [17]Now after several years I came to bring alms to my nation and to present offerings. [18]While I was doing this, they found me purified in the temple, without any crowd or tumult. But some Jews from Asia—[19]they ought to be here before you and to make an accusation, should they have anything against me. [20]Or else let these men themselves say what wrongdoing they found when I stood before the council, [21]other than this one thing that I cried out while standing among them: 'It is with respect to the resurrection of the dead that I am on trial before you this day.'"

[22]But Felix, having a rather accurate knowledge of the Way, put them off, saying, "When Lysias the tribune comes down, I will decide your case." [23]Then he gave orders to the centurion that he should be kept in custody but have some liberty, and that none of his friends should be prevented from attending to his needs.

[24]After some days Felix came with his wife Drusilla, who was Jewish, and he sent for Paul and heard him speak about faith in Christ Jesus. [25]And as he reasoned about righteousness and self-control and the coming judgment, Felix was alarmed and said, "Go away for the present. When I get an opportunity I will summon you." [26]At the same time he hoped that money would be given him by Paul. So he sent for him often and conversed with him. [27]When two years had elapsed, Felix was succeeded by Porcius Festus. And desiring to do the Jews a favor, Felix left Paul in prison. [emphasis added]

WHEN?[3]

Paul, the Jewish Zealot, was converted to Christianity in AD 36 (Acts 9:3–9). The high priest was able to have Stephen stoned without permission of the Roman authorities (Acts 7:58) because the position of imperial procurator in Palestine was vacant. The Roman governor of Syria appointed Jonathan high priest and allowed him independent rule in Palestine (Josephus, *Antiquities* 18:90, 95) during the interregnum of AD 36. Because of this, Jonathan could authorize the stoning of Stephen and sign letters for Saul/Paul to carry to Damascus to persecute and arrest Christians[4] Thus the martyrdom of Stephen and conversion of Paul occurred in AD 36. After being baptized in Damascus (Acts 9:18), Paul remained in the Syrian desert outside Damascus, which was occupied by Nabateans (which is why he called it "Arabia"), until returning to the city (Acts 9:22; Galatians 1:17). Jews sought his demise, and he escaped to Jerusalem (Acts 9:23; 2 Corinthians 11:32–33).

But Paul was not accepted there. "And when he had come to Jerusalem, he attempted to join the disciples. And they were all afraid of him, for they did not believe that he was a disciple" (Acts 9:26). Barnabas was instrumental in changing this.

---

3   I am completely dependent upon Reicke for all New Testament dating and historical evidence for the same, unless otherwise noted. Dating the New Testament events and books is a labyrinth of complexity. Reicke's work is coherent, compelling, scholarly, and respects the integrity of the New Testament. There are, of course, several other dating possibilities that take seriously the text's own claims to integrity (e.g., F. F. Bruce). See L. C. A. Alexander, "Chronology of Paul" in *Dictionary of Paul and His Letters* (Downers Grove, IL: InterVarsity Press, 1993), 115ff.

4   Reicke, *Re-examining*, 35.

Barnabas

Barnabas is first introduced to us in the fourth chapter of Acts. "Thus Joseph, who was also called by the apostles Barnabas (which means son of encouragement), a Levite, a native of Cyprus, sold a field that belonged to him and brought the money and laid it at the apostle's feet" (Acts 4:36–37). Barnabas demonstrated the appropriateness of his apostolic nickname through this generous offering and his efforts to gain Paul's acceptance in Jerusalem, "But Barnabas took him [Paul] and brought him to the apostles and declared to them how on the road he had seen the Lord, who spoke to him, and how at Damascus he had preached boldly in the name of Jesus. So he went in and out among them at Jerusalem, preaching boldly in the name of the Lord" (Acts 9:27–28).

In Galatians 1:18, Paul indicates that he went to Jerusalem three years after he was converted. As Reicke points out, since it was the custom to include both the (partial) initial and concluding years in the whole, Paul actually went to Jerusalem after two years, and visited Peter "fifteen days" (Galatians 1:18) in AD 38.[5] Paul then fled under threat to Tarsus (Acts 9:30) via Caesarea.

Barnabas was sent from Jerusalem to Antioch to deal with the influx of Gentiles as a result of the preaching of those who scattered in the wake of Stephen's martyrdom (Acts 11:19–20).[6] Most spoke "the word to no one except Jews. But there were some of them, men of Cyprus and Cyrene, who on coming to Antioch spoke to the Hellenists also, preaching the Lord Jesus" (Acts 11:19–20). "A great number who believed turned to the Lord" (v. 21). Barnabas retrieved Paul from Tarsus and brought him to Antioch, where they taught for "a whole year" (v. 26).

A famine occurred in Palestine about AD 46.[7] The "prophets [who] came down from Jerusalem" (Acts 11:27) included one Agabus, who foretold the

---

5 This corresponds to the reign of Nabatean King Aretas IV (9 BC–AD 38), whom Paul mentioned with respect to his escape from Damascus (2 Corinthians 11:32–33).

6 Was Paul of specific interest to Barnabas and the Jerusalem Church because of his former unblemished status as a Jewish Zealot? Perhaps in choosing Paul, they hoped to satisfy the zealotic elements within the church.

7 Reicke notes Josephus, *Antiquities* 3:320–21; 20:51–53, 111. Suetonius mentioned recurring food shortages during the reign of Claudius (44–48). Nickle notes a study by Jeremias that demonstrated that AD 47–48 was a Sabbath year in which fields lay fallow, thus increasing the negative impact of draught and

coming famine, which Luke writes occurred during the reign of Emperor Claudius (41–54).[8] "So the disciples determined, everyone according to his ability, to send relief to the brothers living in Judea. And they did so, sending it to the elders by the hand of Barnabas and Saul" (11:29–30). This occurred then, in AD 46. Jerusalem was particularly susceptible to such famine. Its soil is generally poor-quality clay. It possessed really only one natural water source (the spring of Shiloach). While the city had access to several ports, the roads were poor. The temple generated a tremendous volume of trade. Foreign trade consisted mainly of food, clothing, precious metals, and luxury goods. Chief imports were wheat, oil, and livestock.[9] Jerusalem enjoyed a generally higher standard of living, but the cost of living was also higher than the rest of the country.[10] In times of famine and drought, prices skyrocketed. There were only two grains (barley and wheat) grown in the region, and the wheat crop was particularly prone to fluctuation.[11]

The significance of this "protocollection" for the later great collection of Paul cannot be overestimated. The preaching of the Gospel to the Gentiles in Antioch is the first explicit reference to actual mission activity among non-Jews in Acts. The sending of Barnabas indicated concern on the part of the Jerusalem Church. Barnabas was greatly moved and impressed, however, by these new Christians (Acts 11:23). Paul and Barnabas saw in the gathering of a collection for the suffering Church in Jerusalem (and perhaps for Christians more broadly in Palestine) a golden opportunity for practical expression of not only goodwill but also of unity in the Gospel. The significant elements of the later great collection are present in Acts 11:29.

---

famine (31). See Keith F. Nickle, *The Collection: A Study in Paul's Strategy* (London: SCM Press, 1966), 29.

8   Nickle, *The Collection*, 29. Le Cornu and Shulam note that the entire decade of the forties was beset with famine and shortage, although determining what caused these grain shortages and their extent is difficult due to the wide variety in the literature (p. 628). Le Cornu and Shulam discuss the time frame in which the effects of famine were being felt in the Holy Land and some of the possible contributing factors. See Hilary Le Cornu with Joseph Shulam, *A Commentary on the Jewish Roots of Acts* (Jerusalem: Academon, 2003), 629.

9   Le Cornu, *A Commentary*, 630–31.

10   Le Cornu, *A Commentary*, 632.

11   Le Cornu and Shulam discuss the effect of disturbances to the production or transportation of agricultural products, and the results of the sabbatical year. See Le Cornu, *A Commentary*, 633.

1. The collection is a communal act (not simply the act of interested individuals): "So the disciples determined."

2. The collection is taken up among individuals without coercion or legalistic prescriptions: "every one according to his ability."

3. The collection is called a "diakonian," or service.

4. The collection is for the "brothers living in Judea."

5. The collection is a corporate churchly act with respect to both its delivery and reception: "And they did so, sending it to the elders by the hand of Barnabas and Saul."

DISCUSSION QUESTIONS 1

Describe a disaster that impacted you or someone you know. What kinds of relief were needed? Who provided them?

_____

_____

_____

Why might a Christian community choose to direct their aid to Christian brothers and sisters in need rather than to all the victims, believers and unbelievers alike?

_____

_____

_____

What benefits come out of the whole congregation or community joining together in a collection rather than just a few interested individuals?

_____

_____

_____

Thereafter (AD 47), the Church in Antioch sent Paul and Barnabas to Cyprus (Acts 13:1, 3, 4, 13) and through Pisidian Antioch into Asia Minor (Acts 13:1–14:28; Cyprus, Pamphylia, Pisidian Antioch, Iconium, Lystra, Syrian Antioch). Thus Paul's first missionary journey occurred in the years 47–48.[12] The Gentile problem, which needed Barnabas's attention earlier, was only growing as a result of this missionary work. After disagreements with emissaries from Jerusalem back in Antioch, the Church in Antioch resolved to send Paul and Barnabas "to go up to Jerusalem to the apostles and the elders about this question" (Acts 15:2). "I went up again to Jerusalem with Barnabas, taking Titus along with me" (Galatians 2:1). (More on the significant role of Titus in the collection below.)[13] This assumes, as most scholars agree, that the account of Acts 15 (the apostolic council, also called the Jerusalem Council) and the account related by Paul in Galatians 2:1–14 are one and the same event.[14]

After the letter was brought by Paul and Barnabas from Jerusalem back to Antioch, "Paul and Barnabas remained in Antioch, teaching and preaching the word of the Lord, with many others also" (Acts 15:35). The next verse indicates the stay was short: "And after some days Paul said to Barnabas, 'Let us return and visit the brothers in every city where we proclaimed the word of the Lord, and see how they are'" (v. 36) A disagreement ensued over John Mark, and the two split. "Paul chose Silas and departed, having been commended by the brothers to the grace of the Lord. And he went through Syria and Cilicia, strengthening the churches" (vv. 40–41) This second missionary journey of Paul (Acts 15:36–18:22) thus commenced toward the end of AD 49 or beginning of AD 50. Reicke suggests that Paul is active in Asia Minor in AD 50–51 and spent the end of 51 and beginning of AD 52 in Macedonia (16:11). Paul may have returned to Antioch from Corinth (18:18–22) in the spring and summer of 54.[15]

It is at first somewhat surprising that there is no mention of any collection on the second journey or a delivery of funds to Jerusalem at its end.

---

12 Reicke, *Re-examining*, 36.

13 Reicke discusses Galatians 2:1, where Paul mentions coming up to Jerusalem "after fourteen years." See Reicke, *Re-examining*, 36.

14 Reicke, *Re-examining*, 17.

15 Reicke, *Re-examining*, 36.

Acts 18:22 states with tantalizing brevity, "When he had landed in Caesarea, he went up and greeted the church, and then went down to Antioch." There is no mention of any delegation with Paul as he ends his second journey (unlike that indicated in Paul's third journey—Acts 20:1–21:17). But that there was no significant collection on the second journey makes some sense. This was Paul's first visit to numerous communities (Macedonia), and he was surely reticent to push hard for funds, which is completely in keeping with the apostle's known demeanor (Acts 20:34–35). Acts 16:4 does record that "as they went on their way through the cities, they delivered to them for observance the decisions that had been reached by the apostles and elders who were in Jerusalem." Certainly, Paul was laying the groundwork also for honoring Galatians 2:10, "to remember the poor." This concern would in fact become Paul's "obsession."[16] It is most likely, however, that the food crisis of the late forties in Palestine had temporarily subsided.

The third missionary journey (Acts 18:23–21:15) began soon after Paul's return to Antioch, presumably in AD 54. "After spending some time there, he departed and went from one place to the next through the region of Galatia and Phrygia, strengthening all the disciples" (Acts 18:23). It was the third journey that Paul used extensively for the Jerusalem collection. Beginning the journey in 54, he preached in Ephesus in 55–56 (19:8–10). Paul's preaching was so successful he was cutting into the business of the idol manufacturers there, and a riot ensued. Paul then immediately "departed for Macedonia" (20:1), and then proceeded to Greece (Corinth) for "three months" (20:3) during the winter of AD 57–58. Shortly before Easter (Acts 20:6), Paul returned from Macedonia, reaching Jerusalem in the summer of AD 58.[17]

References to the collection in the Pauline corpus coincide with the overall dating of the letters of Paul. The letters that mention the collection are Galatians (2:10); 1 Corinthians (16:1–4); 2 Corinthians (8–9); and

---

16 McKnight concludes that the suggestion of the Jerusalem leaders in Galatians 2:10 became Paul's obsession. S. McKnight, "Collection for the Saints" in *Dictionary of Paul and His Letters* (Downers Grove, IL: InterVarsity Press, 1993), 143.

17 Reicke, *Re-examining*, 36–37.

Romans (15:25). These letters are most convincingly dated within the period of the third missionary journey. Reicke's dating is as follows:

EARLY PALESTINIAN JEWISH—JEWISH CHRISTIAN TENSION

1. 2 Thessalonians (Summer AD 52)

2. 1 Thessalonians (AD 52/53)

RISING ZEALOTISM [PERIOD OF THE GREAT COLLECTION]

3. Galatians (AD 55); written from Ephesus

4. 1 Corinthians (Spring AD 56); written from Ephesus

5. 1 Timothy (Summer/Fall AD 56); written in Macedonia

6. 2 Corinthians (Summer AD 57); written in Macedonia

7. Romans (early AD 58); written during Paul's three-month stay in Corinth

8. Titus (AD 58); sent to Titus in Crete as Paul sailed to Jerusalem

PAUL'S CAPTIVITY

9. Philemon (AD 59)

10. Colossians (AD 59)

11. Ephesians (AD 59)

12. 2 Timothy (AD 60)

13. Philippians (AD 61/62)[18]

---

18 Reicke, Re-examining, 141.

Significant Texts and Dates from Acts for the Third Missionary Journey

• "And he stayed a year and six months [in Corinth on the second journey] teaching the word of God" (Acts 18:11). [AD 51–52]

• "But when Gallio was proconsul of Achaia, the Jews made a united attack on Paul" (Acts 18:12). [AD 51–52][19]

• "When he had landed in Caesarea, he went up and greeted the church, and then went down to Antioch. After spending some time there, he departed and went from one place to the next through the region of Galatia and Phrygia" (Acts 18:22–23). [AD 54]

• "While Apollos was at Corinth, Paul passed through the inland country and came to Ephesus" (19:1). [AD 55]

• "He entered the synagogue and for three months spoke boldly" (19:8).

• "When some became stubborn . . ., he withdrew . . ., reasoning daily in the hall of Tyrannus" (19:9).

• "This continued for two years, so that all the residents of Asia heard the word" (19:10). [AD 55–56] Paul writes Galatians.[20] Paul writes 1 Corinthians: "But I will stay in Ephesus until Pentecost" (1 Corinthians 16:8). Directions for the collection in 1 Corinthians 16:1–4.

• "After the uproar [of the silversmith Demetrius in Ephesus] ceased, Paul sent for the disciples, and after encouraging them, he said farewell and departed for Macedonia. When he had gone through those regions and had given them much encouragement, he came to Greece. There he spent three months" (20:1–3). [Winter AD 57–58] Paul writes Romans (Collection—Romans

---

19 Reicke notes archaeological evidence for these dates. Reicke, *Re-examining*, 36.

20 Reicke explains a possible connection between the Zealots and Peter's about-face in Antioch (Galatians 2:11–13). Reicke, *Re-examining*, 47.

15:25–28). Since Paul mentions his intention to leave for Jerusalem with the collection in the last chapters of Romans, it is most likely he wrote this famous epistle during his three months in Corinth.[21]

- [Paul travels to Illyricum sometime before arriving in Corinth.] "From Jerusalem and all the way around to Illyricum I have fulfilled the ministry of the gospel of Christ" (Romans 15:19). [Late AD 57]

- "He decided to return through Macedonia" (20:3).

- "We sailed away from Philippi after the days of Unleavened Bread, and in five days we came to them at Troas, where we stayed for seven days" (Acts 20:6). [Easter AD 58]

- "On the first day of the week, when we were gathered together to break bread" (Acts 20:7). [First Sunday after Easter AD 58]

- "We set sail for Assos, intending to take Paul aboard there, for so he had arranged, intending himself to go by land. And when he met us as Assos, we took him on board and went to Mitylene" (20:13–14).

- "And sailing from there we came the following day opposite Chios; the next day we touched at Samos; and the day after that we went to Miletus. For Paul had decided to sail past Ephesus, so that he might not have to spend time in Asia, for he was hastening to be at Jerusalem, if possible, on the day of Pentecost" (20:15–16). Paul writes Titus while sailing to Jerusalem [AD 58].

- "From Miletus he sent to Ephesus and called the elders of the church to come to him" (20:17).

- "And when we had parted from them [the Ephesian elders] and set sail, we came by a straight course to Cos, and the next day to Rhodes, and from there to Patara. And having found a ship

---

21 Reicke, Re-examining, 63.

crossing to Phoenicia, we went aboard and set sail. When we had come in sight of Cyprus, leaving it on the left we sailed to Syria and landed at Tyre, for there the ship was to unload its cargo. And having sought out the disciples, we stayed there for seven days. And through the Spirit they were telling Paul not to go on to Jerusalem. When our days there were ended, we departed and went on our journey. . . . Then we went on board the ship. . . . When we had finished the voyage from Tyre, we arrived at Ptolemais, and we greeted the brothers and stayed with them for one day. On the next day we departed and came to Caesarea, and we entered the house of Philip the evangelist, who was one of the seven, and stayed with him" (21:1–8). It is quite significant that Paul stays with "one of the seven" in charge of *diakonia* for the needy.

DISCUSSION QUESTIONS 2

The apostles appointed the seven in Acts 6:1–6 to oversee the distribution of contributions among the Christians in Jerusalem. Why is it significant that Paul stayed with one of these seven on his way to Jerusalem?

_____

_____

_____

If your congregation or a group of neighboring congregations was raising a collection for the congregations in an area of need, what value would you expect to find in communicating with the disaster response arm of LCMS World Relief and Human Care?

_____

_____

_____

- "After these days we got ready and went up to Jerusalem. And some of the disciples from Caesarea went with us, bringing us to the house of Mnason of Cyprus, an early disciple, with whom we should lodge" (Acts 21:15–16).

- "When we had come to Jerusalem, the brothers received us gladly. On the following day Paul went in with us to James, and all the elders were present. After greeting them, he related one by one the things that God had done among the Gentiles through his ministry [*diakonias*]" (Acts 21:17–19). [Around Pentecost AD 58]

- "Then the tribune came up and arrested him" (Acts 21:33).

- "When they had come to Caesarea and delivered the letter to the governor [Felix], they presented Paul also before him" (Acts 23:33). "Now after several years I came to bring alms [*elenmosunas*] to my nation and to present offerings [*prosphoras*]" (Acts 24:17).

- "Then he [Felix] gave orders . . . that he [Paul] should be kept in custody" (Acts 24:23). [AD 58–60]

- "When two years had elapsed, Felix was succeeded by Porcius Festus. And desiring to do the Jews a favor, Felix left Paul in prison" (Acts 24:27).[22]

- "'I appeal to Caesar.' Then Festus, when he had conferred with his council, answered, 'To Caesar you have appealed; to Caesar you shall go'" (Act 25:11–12).

22 For a discussion of the reasons for Felix's indecisiveness regarding Paul, see Reicke, *Re-examining*, 38.

JEWISH CULTURAL CONTEXT AT THE TIME OF THE COLLECTION

In the period of the collection, the cultural context was one of rising conflict between Palestinian Zealots and the Roman government. This also meant rising tensions between Jews and Gentiles and between Jewish and Gentile Christians. At the end of Claudius's reign, he had expelled the Jews from Rome. "As the Jews were indulging in constant riots at the instigation of Chrestus, he banished them from Rome" (Dio Cassius, *History* 60.6). The tumult that caused expulsion was likely the internal Jewish debate about Christ.[23] As a result, Aquila and Priscilla were expelled and found refuge in Corinth, where they met Paul on his third journey. Claudius (41–54) had generally left the Jews alone, and so did Nero (54–68), at least in his early years as ruler.[24] The ruling establishment viewed the Jewish/Jewish Christian matter as an internal affair over fine points of religious custom and preferred not be involved unless tumult and riot resulted.

Palestinian Jews generally detested Roman sovereignty, but the political intrigue involved with such occupation is as complex as that of modern Palestine. Since the Zealots did not distinguish between politics and religion, they were deeply interested in the reassertion of strict Jewish observance.[25] They were Jewish nationalists. They hoped to oust Roman rule by way of guerilla tactics, striking especially those Jews who were favorably disposed to the governing establishment.[26] Roman rule brought

---

23   F. F. Bruce, *Commentary on the Book of Acts* (Grand Rapids: Eerdmans, 1954), 368.

24   Emperor Claudius upheld the rights of Jews to continue the religious customs of their ancestors, but denied them the right of Roman citizenship. See Wayne A. Meeks, *The First Urban Christians* (New Haven: Yale University Press, 1983). 38.

25   F. F. Bruce, *Apostle of the Heart Set Free* (Grand Rapids: Eerdmans, 1977), 28.

26   *The Works of Josephus*, trans. William Whiston (Peabody, MA: Hendrickson Publishers, 1987), 535. Josephus, *Antiquities*, 20:160, 164.

Roman and Greek influences into Palestine, which the Zealots detested. Of course, there was a strong overlapping of Zealot and Pharisaic movements. Thus St. Paul had been both a Zealot and Pharisee. "A Hebrew of Hebrews; as to the law, a Pharisee; as to zeal, a persecutor of the church; as to righteousness under the law, blameless" (Philippians 3:5–6). Nero was particularly fond of Hellenism (Greek custom and influence) and brought such Hellenism to bear in Palestine—including the attempt to put his own statue in the temple—which inflamed the Zealots to new levels of terror and killing.[27] The period of zealotism is decisively capped with the destruction of Jerusalem in 66 and the first Jewish war (66–70). The period from the death of Christ to the destruction of the temple is marked by intense Jewish animosity and persecution of Christians. The Book of Galatians, along with numerous references in the Book of Acts, indicates that during the years of the collection (54–58), there was also significant pro-Jewish/nationalist sentiment within the Christian community. By maintaining Jewish identity in Palestine, Christians, to some extent, avoided Zealot persecution. When Paul visited James in Jerusalem, the latter made a comment that indicates the nature of the challenge faced particularly with the Galatians. "You see, brother, how many thousands there are among the Jews of those who have believed. They are all zealous for the law, and they have been told about you that you teach all the Jews who are among the Gentiles to forsake Moses, telling them not to circumcise their children or walk according to our customs" (Acts 21:20–21). Soon after this account, Paul is arrested in the temple. Were these zealotic Jewish Christians, at least in part, the cause of Paul's arrest? Perhaps so. This was the context to which Paul brought his collection and which ended in his arrest. The problem of Jewish Christian and Gentile Christian relationships within one church was acute.

---

27   Reicke, Re-examining, 37.

DISCUSSION QUESTIONS 3

Name some of the issues that divide congregations today.

_____

_____

_____

How have you seen such divisions hamper a congregation's ministry?

_____

_____

_____

WHO?

We shall limit the "Who?" to those mentioned in 2 Corinthians and the list of traveling companions in Acts 20.

1. "Paul, an apostle of Christ Jesus" (2 Corinthians 1:1).

2. "and Timothy our brother" (1:1).

3. "To the church of God that is at Corinth" (1:1).

4. "with all the saints who are in the whole of Achaia" (1:1).

5. "the churches of Macedonia" (8:1).

6. "Accordingly, we urged Titus" (8:6).

7. The poor in Jerusalem: "supplying the needs of the saints" (9:12).

Paul

"Paul, an apostle of Christ Jesus" (1:1). "I am a Jew, from Tarsus in Cilicia, a citizen of no obscure city" (Acts 21:39). Paul is a man caught by the Gospel between two worlds. He has impeccable Jewish and Zealot credentials (Philippians 3), and yet he is the apostle to the Gentiles. From Zealot persecutor of Christians to zealous advocate of Gentile Christianity, Paul is the ideal apostle for the transition from Jewish Christianity to Christianity beyond an ethnic enclave. He knows the former, has a thoroughgoing Jewish pedigree, yet has the vision and force of personality and conviction to take the Gospel where it must go according to Christ's own mandate, "to the end of the earth" (Acts 1:8). He was a man made for the moment, raised in cosmopolitan Tarsus, familiar with the literature of non-Jewish antiquity.

"This man is a Roman citizen" (Acts 22:26). Paul was born a citizen, and that means his father was a Roman citizen. Given the laws for citizenship, it is likely that either Paul's father or a grandfather performed some outstanding act of service for the state and received citizenship as a reward. A tentmaker might have been extremely useful to a proconsul executing war.[28] Paul knew Roman law and took advantage of it for his purposes (Acts 22:26–29). When Paul describes himself as a "Hebrew of Hebrews," it is to be taken in a narrower sense than merely "an ethnic Jew." The services in Hebrew synagogues were in Hebrew, while Aramaic was used for normal speaking. Hellenistic (or ethnic) Jews used Greek scriptures and prayers.[29] Raised an Orthodox Jew in Tarsus, Paul was sent to Jerusalem by his parents early on. He could later state of Jerusalem that he "was brought up in this city, educated at the feet of Gamaliel" (Acts 22:3). By his own account, Paul was "a Pharisee, a son of Pharisees" (Acts 23:6). Gamaliel was the leading Pharisee of his day. The Pharisees had risen as a party within Judaism particularly during the struggles in the second century BC against the Ptolemies and Seleucids. The younger generation regarded the Pharisees as stubborn and outdated, resisting new religious ideas.[30]

Timothy

Timothy is the co-author of 2 Corinthians (1:1). Timothy had worked extensively with Paul in Ephesus, and Paul directed Timothy to remain there as pastor while he traveled to Macedonia (1 Timothy 1:3). This was in AD 56–57. In the spring of 56, Timothy carried Paul's first letter through Macedonia to Corinth. He was accompanied by Erastus and some others (Acts 19:22; 1 Corinthians 4:17; 16:10).[31] That letter gives specific directives regarding the collection and indications of Paul's intent regarding the collection. Paul introduces the matter as one that is known already to the Corinthians: "Now concerning the collection for the saints" (16:1). He indicates that he has given the same directive to Galatia: "as I directed the churches of Galatia, so you also are to do" (v. 1). Paul advises that each

---

28 Bruce, *Apostle of the Heart,* 37.
29 Bruce, *Apostle of the Heart,* 42.
30 Bruce, *Apostle of the Heart,* 45.
31 Reicke, *Re-examining,* 108.

is to give a gift on Sunday, which is to be stored up, so there will be no collection when he comes (v. 2). The Corinthians will "accredit by letter" those who will carry the gift to Jerusalem (v. 3). Verse 4 ends with a bit of feigned humility: "If it seems advisable that I should go also, they will accompany me." Paul's letter, sent by Timothy's hand, gives this directive: "When Timothy comes, see that you put him at ease among you, for he is doing the work of the Lord" (v. 10). What precisely is that work? Among other things—straightening out the many conflicts in Corinth—that work was assisting in organizing the collection. Paul urged that Timothy be sent back to Ephesus soon (1 Corinthians 16:11). Timothy took over the ministry in Ephesus, while Paul proceeded to Macedonia, working hard there for the sake of the collection. Reicke suggests quite convincingly that 1 Timothy is a letter directed to Timothy and the entire Ephesian Christian community (commending Timothy, speaking of his ordination, commission, leadership for the sake of the community).[32] One year later, Timothy joined Paul in Macedonia as the co-author of 2 Corinthians (1:1). Reicke points out the extremely frequent use of "we" instead of "I" in that letter.[33] The many references in 2 Corinthians to suffering by the apostle and Timothy ("we") are references to the intense persecution experienced especially by Timothy at the hands of the Jew Alexander in Ephesus,[34] before he joined Paul in Macedonia (Acts 19:33; 1 Timothy 1:20; 2 Timothy 4:14; Acts 19:23–27; 1 Timothy 1:7; 4:3). The problems in Ephesus caused Paul not to visit on his trip to Jerusalem, but only to meet the elders in Miletus (Acts 20). Timothy worked extensively with Paul on all aspects of the collection and spent time in both Corinth and Macedonia, as well as Ephesus. It is unclear whether he accompanied Paul to Jerusalem with the collection.

Timothy was a very appropriate selection for Paul. He was thoroughly conversant with Judaism via his mother and grandmother. Eunice and Lois had been pious Jews (2 Timothy 1:5). He had a tremendous reputation in

---

32 Reicke, Re-examining, 108.

33 Reicke, Re-examining, 109.

34 Virtually every Mediterranean city had a significant Jewish population in the first century. The Diaspora that resulted from the sixth century BC Babylonian conquest of Palestine resulted in an estimated five or six million Diaspora Jews by the first century. See Meeks, The First Urban Christians, 34.

his hometown, Lystra. Timothy's father was a Greek. Paul had Timothy circumcised because (unlike the Gentile Titus) Timothy, in traveling with Paul, would have been expected to be and act as a Jew. According to Acts 16, Paul and Timothy traveled though the cities of Asia publishing the decision of the apostolic council, which included the directive recorded in Galatians to "remember the poor." Since Galatians was written on the third journey, that letter itself provides the very evidence that the collection was part of Paul's message (Galatians 2:10) in Asia. Timothy was an ideal choice in Paul's quest for the collection to bridge the gulf between Gentile and Jewish Christianity. He was extremely loyal and knew the apostle's mind (1 Corinthians 4:17). First Timothy was written by Paul to Timothy and the Church in Ephesus from Macedonia (site of Paul's most successful work for the collection). Second Corinthians (with its most extensive discussion of the collection) was written by Paul with Timothy from Macedonia. Romans mentions the collection and that Timothy (16:21) was present with Paul when it was written. Timothy accompanied Paul with the collection to Jerusalem (Acts 20:4).

The Church of God That Is in Corinth

It is rather astounding that Paul is so adamant about the collection in addressing the Corinthians. That the congregation held the potential for significant contributions cannot be the final cause of his intensity. The fact that he did so demonstrates, I believe, how fundamentally theological and significant the collection is for him. It is not simply an adiaphorous matter that can easily be ignored. I would not be prone to cajole a very troubled congregation about a collection. But it is precisely the genius of the apostle to emphasize the theological nature of the collection, catechizing the Corinthians to look outside themselves and their immediate problems, while aiming for nearly the same effect with the recipients of the collection.

DISCUSSION QUESTIONS 4

How can a congregation benefit from collecting gifts that will leave the area and be sent to other Christians far away?

_____

_____

_____

Recipients of our collections clearly benefit in material ways. How do they also benefit spiritually or theologically?

_____

_____

_____

The Corinthian congregation had been founded by Paul on his second journey (Acts 18) after a trip to Athens. Corinth was the capital city of Achaia, and the city was placed advantageously at the intersection of trade routes of land and sea. The land route connected the Peloponnese and Attica; the two harbors (Lechaeum and Cenchreae) facilitated traffic between the Aegean and Adriatic Seas. It boasted a large temple to Aphrodite. "To Corinthianize" was synonymous with profligate behavior. Corinth was an international city, well known for its wealth, commercial success, and rampant immorality.[35] At the instigation of Caesar after 44 BC, Corinth grew as a colony of Italian citizens, but it saw a steady influx of Greeks and Eastern peoples (including Jews) who worked as entrepreneurs in the city (thus Paul worked for Aquila in the city; Acts 18:2–3).[36] Meeks suggests the Corinthian Christians were not excessively wealthy, but more likely the typical artisans and tradespeople. He bases this on Paul's advice that the collection is to be assembled little by little, week by week (1 Corinthians 16:1–4).[37]

---

35 Bo Reicke, _The New Testament Era: The World of the Bible from 500 B.C. to 100 A.D._, trans. David Green (Philadelphia: Fortress Press, 1968), 233.

36 Reicke, _The New Testament Era_, 233.

37 Meeks, _The First Urban Christians_, 65.

The problems in the congregation were numerous. Paul responded at length in 1 Corinthians to a letter sent from the congregation. There were several extant fissures threatening to split the congregation apart (1:12–16).[38] Theologians of glory boasted of strength, wisdom, and miracles. There were problems of sexual immorality, lawsuits between Christians (an indication of means),[39] marriage, food offered to idols, attacks on the apostle himself, misuse of the Lord's Supper, the role of women in worship, order in worship, prophecy and interpretation, and the resurrection of Christ and of the dead in general. Despite the long list of problems dealt with in the letter, Paul praised the Corinthians for their tremendous gifts of knowledge and speech (1 Corinthians 1:4–7). At the end of the long letter, he turns to the collection with a characteristic "Now concerning" (*Peri de*), indicating that the Corinthians themselves had raised the issue in their letter to the apostle.[40] The directions are matter-of-fact and brief. There seems to be no controversy among the Corinthians over the matter, or at least none that they had raised in their (now lost) letter to Paul.

1. Now concerning the collection [*logeias*] for the saints: as I directed the churches of Galatia, so you also are to do. (1 Corinthians 16:1)

2. On the first day of every week, each of you is to put something aside and store it up, as he may prosper, so that there will be no collecting [*logeiai*] when I come. (v. 2)

3. And when I arrive, I will send those whom you accredit by letter to carry your gift to Jerusalem. (v. 3)

4. If it seems advisable that I should go also, they will accompany me. (v. 4)

---

38 Meeks, *The First Urban Christians*, 65.

39 Meeks, *The First Urban Christians*, 66. Though what level of "means" is unclear. Meeks cites papyri which indicate village farmers and small traders appeared before magistrates in opposition to their neighbors.

40 See the documentary evidence in Nickle that Paul had already introduced his collection project to the Corinthians (see 1 Corinthians 16:1–4) and they, in turn, had asked questions about it. Keith F. Nickle, *The Collection: A Study in Paul's Strategy* (London: SCM Press, 1966), 15.

The Churches of Macedonia

Paul indicates that the Macedonian Christians gave to the collection despite their "extreme poverty" (2 Corinthians 8:2). The Macedonian parishes were particularly those of Berea, Thessalonica, and Philippi. Achaia had belonged to Macedonia from 147 to 27 BC. Caesar Augustus elevated Achaia to its own province because of the rising importance of Corinth. In AD 15–44, it was joined again to Macedonia. In AD 44, Claudius divided them into two senatorial provinces.[41] Achaia outshone Macedonia both with respect to its capital (Corinth) and its intellectual center (Athens).[42] The churches had been founded on Paul's second missionary journey (Acts 16:6–10; 2 Corinthians 2:12–13). Paul finds an opportunity for his rhetorical skill in using opposites to describe the situation faced by the Macedonians, who nevertheless gave generously. "For in a severe test of affliction, their abundance of joy and their extreme poverty have overflowed in a wealth of generosity on their part" (2 Corinthians 8:2).[43]

"With All the Saints Who Are in the Whole of Achaia"
(2 Corinthians 1:1)

While the Corinthians were a constant problem, the Christians of Achaia had an unblemished relationship with Paul, and they seem not to have been affected by the problems of their province's most famous congregation. In fact, the Achaians had an excellent reputation in general in the ancient world. While Corinth was wealthy and cosmopolitan (Julius Caesar had imported eighty thousand Roman settlers, who were mostly freedmen from various ethnic backgrounds), Achaia was largely tribal, Greek, and traditional. Achaia was rural and poor, quiet and largely politically unaffected. Greek Achaia preserved its traditional culture, while Corinth ran after all things new. This was the huge contrast the apostle found between Corinth and the churches of Achaea who were loyal to

---

41 Hans Dieter Betz, *2 Corinthians 8 and 9: A Commentary on Two Administrative Letters of the Apostle Paul*, ed. George W. MacRae (Philadelphia: Fortress Press, 1985), 50.

42 Reicke, *The New Testament Era*, 232.

43 For an insightful explanation of the reasons for the extreme poverty of Macedonia, and Rome's efforts to rejuvenate it, see Betz, *2 Corinthians*, 50.

him.[44] While Paul cajoled the Corinthians to get ready for his visit with respect to the collection, he informed them that in Macedonia, he had praised the Corinthians' fellow Achaians who had been ready with the collection already for a year (2 Corinthians 9:2). If not for the confusion in Corinth, all Achaia would have been ready for the final phase of the collection. But Paul found he could stir the Macedonians to action through the loyal Achaians and rouse the Corinthians by the Macedonians.[45]

Titus

Titus was integrally involved in the entire matter of the collection, from its inception to its practical conclusion. In fact, he was very much personally invested in the matter. When Paul went to Jerusalem for the Apostolic Council in AD 49, Titus accompanied him. "I went up again to Jerusalem with Barnabas, taking Titus along with me" (Galatians 2:1). It was a provocative act by Paul, since Titus was a Gentile, but provocative for the sake of the Gospel. Paul wished to make his point about justification by grace (Galatians 3) and the observance of Mosaic Law, and he made it orally and physically in the person of Titus. "But even Titus, who was with me, was not forced to be circumcised, though he was a Greek" (Galatians 2:3). Pressure to have Titus circumcised was being brought to bear by "false brothers secretly brought in—who slipped in to spy out our freedom that we have in Christ Jesus, so that they might bring us into slavery—to them we did not yield in submission even for a moment, so that the truth of the gospel might be preserved for you" (Galatians 2:4–5).

Who were these "false brothers"? They were certainly individuals affected by the Zealot movement. Nickle finds in Galatians 2:4 ("slipped in") indication that they did not bring their concern to have Titus circumcised directly to Paul, but tried to work James and Peter ("the pillars").[46]

Nickle also goes so far as to assert that these "false brothers" were Jewish infiltrators of the Christian community and not believers.[47] That would

---

44 Betz, *2 Corinthians*, 52.

45 Betz, *2 Corinthians*, 92–93.

46 See Nickle, *The Collection*, 48. Nickle argues that the Zealots infiltrated the vigorously growing Christian church to enlists its members in its nationalistic movement.

47 Nickle, *The Collection*, 48.

accord with Paul's intense rejection of them as "false brothers" (Galatians 2:4). Indeed, Acts 15:1 states, "But some men came down from Judea and were teaching the brothers, 'Unless you are circumcised according to the custom of Moses, you cannot be saved.'" Yet Acts 15:5 clearly calls those who held this position "believers": "But some believers who belonged to the party of the Pharisees rose up and said, 'It is necessary to circumcise them and to order them to keep the law of Moses.'" The apostles and elders gathered and there was "much debate" (Acts 15:7). Some few had gone out, without commission and direction "from us" (Acts 15:24), and advocated the procircumcision position in Antioch, although the apostles and elders "gave them no instructions" to do so (Acts 15:24). Nickle may well be correct about the specific "false brothers" who were the most intense opponents of Paul. They may have been Jewish spies and true Zealots attempting to co-opt the movement. Nevertheless, the Christian community was large. Many priests and Pharisees had joined the group. Zealotism was in the air. It was over the issue of justification by grace (Acts 15:11) and circumcision, and in the very person of Titus, that James and the other Jerusalem leaders decided for grace against the interest of the Zealots (Acts 15:19).

Titus was directly involved with Paul's implementation of the apostolic request of Paul recorded in Galatians, "to remember the poor" (Galatians 2:10). Not appearing in Acts, Titus nevertheless shows up decisively in 2 Corinthians. That means from the events mentioned in Galatians/Acts 15 (written AD 55) that occurred in AD 49, we have no record of Titus with Paul until 2 Corinthians (summer AD 57). The fact that Paul expends almost no ink explaining to the Galatians who Titus is ("though he was a Greek") very likely indicates their familiarity with him (*argumentum a silentio*). The name "Titus" appears eight times in 2 Corinthians, twice in Galatians, once in 2 Timothy, and once in Titus. We learn that Paul expected to find Titus in Troas, where he received the vision inviting him to Macedonia (Acts 16). Yet the apostle complained to the Corinthians, "even though a door was opened for me in the Lord, my spirit was not at rest because I did not find my brother Titus there. So I took leave of them and went on to Macedonia" (2 Corinthians 2:12–13). By AD 57, Titus is a trusted and dear compatriot of the apostle. If 1 Corinthians is the "sorrowful letter" (2 Corinthians 2:1–4), it appears Titus[48] accompanied Timothy in delivering that letter to Corinth. In any case, Paul had sent Titus to Corinth in AD 57, and Titus then returned to Paul in Macedonia, greatly comforting the apostle with positive news from Corinth. Ephesus had been extremely difficult, and though Paul often complimented the Christians in Macedonia, nevertheless, his initial time there was not easy.

> For even when we came into Macedonia, our bodies had no rest, but we were afflicted at every turn—fightings without and fear within. But God, who comforts the downcast, comforted us by the coming of Titus, and not only by his coming but also by the comfort with which he was comforted by you, as he told us of your longing, your mourning, your zeal for me, so that I rejoiced still more. For even if I made you grieve with my letter, I do not regret it—though I did regret it, for I see that that letter grieved you, though only for a while. As it is, I rejoice, not because you were grieved, but because you were grieved into repenting. (2 Corinthians 7:5–9)

After reassuring Paul of the love of the Corinthians, Titus was sent back to Corinth to complete the collection. "We urged Titus that as he had started, so he should complete among you this act of grace" (2 Corinthians 8:6). Soon thereafter, Paul proceeded from Macedonia to Corinth, where he wrote Romans during his three-month stay early in AD 58. Though Paul informed the Romans of the collection (Romans 15:25–28), he did not list Titus among the several compatriots noted in the greeting at the end of the letter (Timothy, Lucius, Jason, Sosipater, Tertius, Gaius, Erastus, Quartus [Romans 16:21–23]). Why? Titus was in Crete, sent there by Paul to put in order that church's leadership. "This is why I left you in Crete, so that you might put what remained into order, and appoint elders in every town as I directed you" (Titus 1:5). The letter to Titus is directed to the churches of Crete, making clear Paul's apostolic commission to Titus to appoint leaders, teach sound doctrine, and urge good works. The letter

---

48   Donald Guthrie, *New Testament Introduction* (Downers Grove, IL: InterVarsity Press, 1970), 435.

finishes those written during the period of the great collection of the third missionary journey.

On his trip to Jerusalem in spring or early summer AD 58, Paul sailed along the west coast of Asia Minor. Along this route, Paul passed a number of places where he would be able to send his letter to Titus in Crete by ship.[49]

Thus Titus is not with Paul when he greets the Ephesian elders (Acts 20), nor does he make the trip to Jerusalem with the apostle. The letter to Titus is short because Paul is aboard ship, or hastily writing to deliver the letter to a boat ready to set sail from an Asian port to Crete. We would expect Paul's last letter of the period of the collection also to make reference to the matter of the collection itself, and we are not disappointed. At the end of the letter, Paul urged Titus to meet him later in Nicopolis (in Epirus, south of Dalmatia and Illyricum), as Paul intended to winter there after taking the collection to Jerusalem—an intention he was unable to fulfill, though Titus did make his way there.[50] The final two verses allude to the collection, which was the "urgent need" in the mind of the apostle. Given the long list of companions on the journey to Jerusalem, the apostle simply says, "All . . . send greetings."

And let our people learn to devote themselves to good works, so as to help cases of urgent need, and not be unfruitful. All who are with me send greetings to you. Greet those who love us in the faith. Grace be with you all. (Titus 3:14–15)

49   Reicke, Re-examining, 68.
50   See 2 Timothy 4:10. Reicke: "Titus's activity in Dalmatia presupposes a stop in that city" (Re-examining, 112).

DISCUSSION QUESTIONS 5

Reread Paul's comments about Titus in 2 Corinthians 7:5–9. What does this show us about the important role Titus played in Paul's ministry?

What are some ways you become a greater source of comfort and encouragement to your pastor?

Sopater, Aristarchus, Secundus, Gaius, Timothy, Tychicus, Trophimus

From the Book of Acts and the Pauline Epistles, we have quite a clear picture of which churches participated in the collection: Galatia (1 Corinthians 16:1); Macedonia (2 Corinthians 8–9); Achaia (Romans 15:26). Sopater (Berea) and Aristarchus and Secundus (Thessalonica) are all from Macedonia. Gaius (Derbe) and Timothy (Lystra) are from Galatia. Tychicus and Trophimus (Ephesus) are from Asia.[51] The author of Acts joined Paul at Philippi, where the author's famous "we" occurs for the first time in the book. "But we sailed away from Philippi after the days of Unleavened Bread" (Acts 20:6). Thus Luke himself was probably a delegate from Philippi or the region.[52] These delegates were the result of Paul's specific directives that each contributing community appoint

---

51 See Nickle, *The Collection*, 68.

52 "*Auch Philippi fehlte unter diesen Gemeinden nicht, weil von Philippi her Lukas wieder mit 'wir' erzaelt. Er blieb von nun an bei Paulus bis zu seinem Tod, 2 Tim. 4:1*," writes Adolf Schlatter, *Die Apostelgeschichte* (Stuttgart: Calwer Verlag, 1948), 244–45.

delegates to take the funds to Jerusalem (1 Corinthians 16:3; 2 Corinthians 8:19–20). Philippi was a strong participant in the collection.[53]

Many have surmised—with good cause—that the list of the delegates presented by Luke is only partial. Does he list only seven as a representative indication of the full delegation, or perhaps a parallel to the seven deacons chosen for the Jerusalem Church in Acts 6?[54] Luke is careful to note, for instance, that "we departed and came to Caesarea, and we entered the house of Philip the evangelist, who was one of the seven, and stayed with him" (Acts 21:8). This first Palestinian contact with Philip was likely both highly practical (Philip was charged with care for the poor; Acts 6:5) and symbolic. Those listed "went on ahead and were waiting for us at Troas." Did an equal or larger number remain behind? Did the seven go on ahead because the small church in Philippi could not accommodate them easily?[55] Georgi suggests that since Paul was able to participate in deciding the course of the ship (Acts 20:13–14; 20:16), "the delegation was quite large and, thus, represented a high percentage of the passengers."[56] Representatives from Achaia and Corinth are not mentioned, despite the fact that Paul had informed the Romans (Romans 15:26) that they were significant contributors.[57] "One can surmise that additional representatives were picked up along the trip. Perhaps delegates were included also from Troas (Acts 20:5, 6bff.), Philippi (Acts 20:6), Tyre (Acts 21:4), Ptolemais (Acts 21:7)—certainly Caesarea, possibly Cyprus (Acts 21:16)."[58]

Betz notes that a number of the names are Latin, making it likely they were Romans.[59] He also notes that the names overlap somewhat with the list in Romans 16:21–23, and perhaps the Romans list is another list of delegates to Jerusalem. Particularly the Macedonian churches were likely

53   Meeks points out that Philippi joined Paul in the collection very early on, and they were generous contributors. Meeks, *The First Urban Christians*, 41.
54   O. Dibelius, referenced by Nickle, *The Collection*, 68, n. 83.
55   So suggests Dieter Georgi, *Remembering the Poor: A History of Paul's Collection for Jerusalem* (Nashville: Abingdon Press, 1992), 123.
56   Georgi, *Remembering the Poor*, 123.
57   Nickle, *The Collection*, 69.
58   Nickle, *The Collection*, 69.
59   Betz, *2 Corinthians*, 51.

to have Roman settlers among them.[60] Such a delegation including Jews would easily be confused by officials for a delegation taking the Diaspora temple tax to Jerusalem and afforded Paul's efforts apparent legal protection (see below).

Paul's specific words to the Ephesian elders might indicate that both delegates and contributions were picked up there at Miletus (Acts 20:17). Thus Paul would have desired to avoid Ephesus (site of so much previous controversy over his preaching) in order to avoid at all costs the danger of zealous locals (Jewish or pagan) accosting him and, more important, the collection itself! Acts 20:34–35 is surely a reference to the collection and an indication of just why the church leaders came to meet him!

> I coveted no one's silver or gold or apparel. You yourselves know that these hands ministered to my necessities and to those who were with me. In all things I have shown you that by working hard in this way we must help the weak and remember the words of the Lord Jesus, how He Himself said, "It is more blessed to give than to receive." (Acts 20:33–35)

Paul had felt compelled to frequently strike the theme that he sought no personal gain from his mission churches precisely because he was collecting funds.[61]

Schlatter is certainly correct in suggesting that no matter how many finally accompanied Paul, the apostle was eager to impress upon the Church in Jerusalem the significance of the Gentile mission and along with its rich financial contribution, its significant numeric strength. The more delegates, the better.[62]

---

60 Betz suggests these men previously had military careers or worked in civilian administration. If so, they might well have had experience both in international travel and in transporting money. Betz, 2 Corinthians, 51–52.

61 Nickle, The Collection, 69.

62 Schlatter, Die Apostelgeschichte, 245.

DISCUSSION QUESTIONS 6

What impact would it make on the struggling Jewish Christians in Jerusalem to see so many Gentile delegates bringing the large relief offering from those other regions?

_____

_____

How is this similar to huge, synodwide collections?

_____

_____

The Poor in Jerusalem
(The Delivery of the Collection)

I have already briefly outlined the general circumstances in Palestine, cultural and political, obtained in the period of the collection. In describing the circumstances of the Antiochene "protocollection," I have also described the general circumstances of famine and its effects on Jerusalem. McKnight suggests several reasons the Jerusalem Church was in a state of particular need:

1. The presence of more and more widows needing care (Acts 6:1–7).

2. Pilgrims to Jerusalem who burdened the community (Acts 2:42-47).

3. Problems from the early community's experimentation with communal life (Acts 4:32–5:11).

4. The economic hardships caused by famine (Acts 11:27–30).

5. Personal stresses due to economic persecution (James 1:9; 2:6–7; 5:1–6).[63]

---

63   McKnight, "Collection for the Saints" in *Dictionary of Paul and His Letters*, 144.

It remains to describe something of the circumstances concerning the reception of the collection. That so very little is mentioned in Acts of the reception is something of a conundrum, given the extraordinary significance of the collection for Paul and the church.[64] Indeed, Luke, as a delegate from Philippi and thereafter lifelong companion of Paul, could hardly have been more involved and interested in the topic. Yet the only specific reference to the collection is made by Paul to Governor Felix, "Now after several years I came to bring alms to my nation and to present offerings" (Acts 24:17). While with one of the seven, Philip the evangelist, in Caesarea, "a prophet named Agabus came down from Judea" (Acts 21:10; the same Agabus who prophesied the famine under Claudius in Acts 11:28?). Paul would be bound and delivered "into the hands of the Gentiles" (Acts 21:11). Upon hearing this, Luke, the delegates, and the locals "urged him not to go up to Jerusalem" (Acts 21:12). Nevertheless, Paul—determined in light of the years of work, the large delegation, and significant amount of money—would not be deterred. The reference Luke gives to the reception by James and the others is certainly veiled.

> **When we had come to Jerusalem, the brothers received us gladly. On the following day Paul went in with us to James, and all the elders were present. After greeting them, he related one by one the things that God had done among the Gentiles through his ministry (*dia tes diakonias*). And when they heard it, they glorified God. (Acts 21:17–19)**

The word translated "ministry" by the ESV is *diakonia*, a technical term Paul used repeatedly for the collection (Romans 15:25; 1 Corinthians 16:15;

---

64 Dr. Jeffrey Oschwald of Concordia Seminary, St. Louis (for whom this paper was written for a graduate course), held that Luke's apparent disinterest in the collection is no more confounding than his lack of detail regarding numerous other issues in the life of the Early Church. If Luke's purpose in writing Acts is to trace the course of the Gospel to Rome (Acts 1:8), then the collection is of less striking significance for Luke. Yet still, for Paul, the collection is in fact evidence of the Gospel's very spread to the end of the earth. "Luke's silence, no doubt, is not explained by recourse to Luke's designs; he obviously did not think descriptions of it were necessary for his purposes. M. Hengel wryly notes that 'Luke does not always say everything that he knows, and when he does, he can mention facts which are important—to us—only in passing' (Hengel, 119)." McKnight, "Collection for the Saints" in *Dictionary of Paul and His Letters*, 144.

2 Corinthians 8:4, 19; 9:1, 12, 13). Immediately, the brothers referenced the delicate political situation and that many believers "are all zealous for the law, and they have been told about you that you teach all the Jews who are among the Gentiles to forsake Moses" (Acts 21:20–21). Paul agreed to a compromise at the suggestion of James and others. He would go with those with him who were Jewish to the temple and undergo the rights of purification.

> Then Paul took the men, and the next day he purified himself along with them and went into the temple, giving notice when the days of purification would be fulfilled and the offering presented for each one of them. (Acts 21:26)

It is a great irony that precisely his willingness to show deference to the Mosaic Law lands him in prison. The wretched Ephesians do him in after all:

> When the seven days were almost completed, the Jews from Asia, seeing him in the temple, stirred up the whole crowd and laid hands on him, crying out, 'Men of Israel, help! This is the man who is teaching everyone everywhere against the people and the law and this place. . . . For they previously had seen Trophimus the Ephesian with him in the city, and they supposed that Paul had brought him into the temple. (Acts 21:27–29)

The Ephesian Jews knew Paul well, and they recognized the Gentile Ephesian delegate Trophimus with Paul. When he warned the Ephesian elders that he was headed for Jerusalem for "imprisonment and afflictions" and that "after my departure fierce wolves will come in among you" (Acts 20:23, 29), he well knew what he was saying. Paul was seized but soon granted a chance on the steps of the temple to address the zealotic crowd. He spoke in Hebrew, he referenced his unblemished Hebrew and Zealot credentials, but his mention that the Lord had said to him, "Go, for I will send you far away to the Gentiles" (Acts 22:21), sent the anti-Hellenist crowd into a rage. His fate was sealed. The collection, the very attempt to overcome the anti-Hellenist animosity of the Jewish Christians, had subjected him to the very epicenter of that animus.[65]

DISCUSSION QUESTIONS 7

Describe a time you did something for someone with the best of intentions but were met with skepticism and condemnation.

_____

_____

_____

What are some things you can do to avoid bitterness and resentment when your generosity is sorely mistreated?

_____

_____

_____

Why is there no fuller account of the collection's delivery, reception, and effects in the final chapters of Acts? This remains somewhat a mystery, though as we have indicated, Luke is not as silent as might be indicated by an initial glance at Acts. Perhaps Paul consciously carried out the collection in the Mediterranean world under the guise of existing laws, which protected the Jewish temple tax and its transmission to Jerusalem. An extensive system was in place for collecting funds for the temple from the Diaspora.

Because the Jews in the Diaspora were so numerous, the amount of contributions flowing annually to the temple was significant. After the temple tax contributions had been collected in the local communities, the custom followed in the Diaspora was to send the funds to central receiving points, from which the large aggregate sums were forwarded to Jerusalem. They were accompanied for protection from banditry by a large retinue consisting of paid mercenary guards, pilgrims, and deputies

---

65 Nickle notes the explosive situation in Jerusalem when Paul delivered the collection. See Nickle, _The Collection_, 147.

from the communities that had contributed, of which the last named were charged with representing the local Jewish fellowship in person at the sacrifices in Jerusalem.[66]

Of numerous possible reasons for the lack of reference to the collection in Acts, most are unsatisfactory, particularly if we accept Acts' own claim to Lukan authorship and accuracy (which we do). It is most likely that by the time Acts was written, the separation between Christianity and Judaism was all but complete, and Luke did not desire to write anything that would unduly bring Roman scrutiny and intrusion to the Christian community. Rome's antagonism for Judaism reached its destructive height and fever pitch in AD 70 with the destruction of the temple. At such a time, it is unlikely that Roman authorities would have looked kindly upon a large collection delivered to the Jews in Judea. It might even have raised suspicions about the Christians, especially if Luke had written a detailed description in Acts.[67]

DISCUSSION QUESTIONS 8

What opportunities can disaster relief provide for Christian missionaries and relief agencies in areas where overt witness is illegal?

---

66   See "Analogies to Paul's Collection in Contemporary Judaism" in Nickle, *The Collection*, 83.

67   Nickle, *The Collection*, 150.

WHAT?

The Account of the Collection in 2 Corinthians 8 and 9

(Commentary)

We now turn to a specific, verse by verse treatment of 2 Corinthians 8 and 9. This section of Paul's letter has long been the subject of historical critical inquiry. Bultmann, of course, among many others, sees no way that chapters 8 and 9 could possibly have been part of the original letter.[68] I have no desire or intent to attempt to unravel the complex issues involved in the assertions that 2 Corinthians is a series of independent letters, genuine or not, cobbled together from numerous sources by some redactor well after the fact. We simply assert with Reicke that 2 Corinthians has a logical coherence as it stands. If it were divided into different writings, that coherence could not be explained.[69]

While he is numbered among those who chop up the letter, Betz provides a magisterial explication of these two chapters based on ancient rhetoric. While perhaps overdone, his rhetorical division of the chapters is nevertheless illuminating, even though we see no real reason to tear these two chapters from the whole as two separate letters by Paul later conflated with other material into 2 Corinthians. Betz also demonstrates that these two chapters are written in highly administrative and even legal style, which coincides with the subject at hand. Where I have made use of Betz or other authors, they are duly noted. Otherwise, ideas are my own.

---

68 Rudolf Bultmann, *The Second Letter to the Corinthians* (Minneapolis: Augsburg, 1976), 18. For the history of interpretation, see Betz, *2 Corinthians*, 3–35.

69 Reicke, *Re-examining*, 61.

8:1–5 The Exordium—Paul seeks to gain the attention of the reader and "put the cards on the table"[70]

8:1 *We want you to know, brothers, about the grace of God that has been given among the churches of Macedonia.* Paul is writing from Macedonia. The Corinthian propensity is to disparage Macedonia as a rural backwater. So Paul quickly gets their attention by noting the example of Macedonia. "Grace" (*charis*) is given by divine action, quite over against works or human activity. Reception of the message of divine favor in Christ has caused something of note among the Macedonians. The Corinthians are well aware of the significance of "grace" in Paul's preaching. It is the strongest and most characteristic term in Paul's theology. Upon it hangs all divine blessing (Galatians 2:21). In fact, chapters 8 and 9 overflow with *charis;*[71] it occurs ten times in these two chapters.

²for in a severe test of affliction, their abundance of joy and their extreme poverty have overflowed in a wealth of generosity on their part. The Macedonians are noteworthy because in a severe trial (*polle dokime thlipsios*) and extreme poverty, their joy in Christ has abounded and resulted in rich giving for the collection. Paul mentions his own physical affliction while in Macedonia (2 Corinthians 7:5—fighting without and fear within), and he must have participated in these difficulties with the Christians there. For Paul, afflictions and trials are always toward positive ends (Romans 8). "Testing" is a significant thread through the eighth chapter (2 Corinthians 8:2, 22) and always provides opportunity for an increase of faith and love. He frequently notes the paradox of joy/affliction. "In all our affliction, I am overflowing with joy" (2 Corinthians 7:4). Generosity (*aplotes*) is for Paul the rich result of faith in Christ and the opposite of greed (*pleonexia*). The generosity flowed as a result of grace.

³For they gave according to their means, as I can testify, and beyond their means, of their own accord. God's grace results in giving beyond one's ability (*dunamin*). Here, Paul introduces a theme that is vital for him in the matter of the collection and of all Christian ethics: "of their own accord." The Gospel suffers no compulsion or coercion (Romans 6:7, 22).

---

70 Betz, *2 Corinthians*, 41.

71 Dunn, *The Theology of Paul the Apostle* (Grand Rapids: Eerdmans, 1998), 710.

[4]*begging us earnestly for the favor of taking part in the relief of the saints*—"With much exertion" (*polles paraklesios*), they plead for the favor (*charis*/grace/gift) even (*kai*) the participation (*koinonia*) in this service/ ministry (*diakonia*). The Macedonians regard the collection as a gift, a privilege. Dunn calls this use of *charis* "transitional." "Charis here seems to signify the (sense of) engracement which prompted the Macedonians to contribute to the collection beyond their means (8:2–23)."[72] *Koinonia* means a partaking of something in common. So Paul can call the Lord's Supper a "participation (*koinonia*) in the blood of Christ" (1 Corinthians 10:16). In Acts 4, the saints have all things in common (*koina*). The very word Paul uses for the Lord's Supper also becomes for him a technical term for the collection. By so sharing in the burdens of the needy saints in Jerusalem, one demonstrates the membership in the Body of Christ.

[5]*and this, not as we expected, but they gave themselves first to the Lord and then by the will of God to us*. "As he [Christ] gives himself for us with his body and blood . . ., so we too are to give ourselves with might and main for our neighbor."[73] Generosity is born of one's relationship to Christ. And service to Christ is rendered by service to the neighbor as a result (Matthew 25:40). To refuse assistance to the neighbor is to refuse Christ.

DISCUSSION QUESTIONS 9

How is the Macedonians' generosity reminiscent of the poor widow who put all she had in the offering box at the temple (Mark 12:42–43)?

_____

_____

How do you balance generosity in offerings (and demonstrating that faith to your family) with being responsible with your family's finances?

_____

_____

---

72 Dunn, *The Theology of Paul*, 707–8.
73 Luther, "Against the Fanatics," LW 36:352

8:6 The Narratio
(Statement of Facts)

⁶*Accordingly, we urged Titus that as he had started, so he should complete among you this act of grace.* As noted above, Titus had been with Paul since Antioch and the visit to Jerusalem in AD 49 for the apostolic council. Paul "urged" (*parakalein*; "exhorted") Titus. The positive action of the Macedonians encouraged Titus to attempt to bring about such positive results among the Corinthians. Titus is to bring the matter to conclusion, to fulfillment (*epiteleo*). Betz notes that while "exhort/urge" (*parakalein*) occurs often in Paul's writing, it is used here in a technical way, to refer to men who are appointed to act as representatives either legally or politically.[74] The flesh would see taking up a collection as an exaction, yet it is forever for Paul an "act of grace." The original simply has "this grace."

8:7–8 The Propositio
(Proposition—Points of Agreement/Disagreement)

⁷*But as you excel in everything—in faith, in speech, in knowledge, in all earnestness, and in our love for you—see that you excel in this act of grace also.* They are flattered by Paul's praise and no doubt agree with it. Paul introduces the very significant term "earnestness" (*spoudeis*). This term signifies for Paul the zealous desire and ability to act freely. This is an important quality both for the Corinthians and their envoys.[75] Paul encourages them by reminding them of his own love for them and encourages them to abound in charitable action as a result of their faith, speech, and knowledge. Without action, all of these are denied.

⁸*I say this not as a command, but to prove by the earnestness of others that your love also is genuine.* Conviction, not coercion, is the goal of the apostle. He will not command (like he would not command celibacy—*epitagen*—1 Corinthians 7:1–6). The zeal of the Macedonians is the occasion for the Corinthians to prove their own fidelity and conviction (faith, zeal, love). Those "accredit[ed] (proved) by letter" (1 Corinthians 16:3) would

---

74   Betz, *2 Corinthians*, 54.
75   Betz, *2 Corinthians*, 58.

represent the Corinthians bearing the collection. Here their act of charity would "accredit" the genuineness (*gnesion*) of their love.

8:9–15 The Probatio
(Proofs—The Deliberative Argument)

The First Proof

⁹For you know the grace of our Lord Jesus Christ, that though He was rich, yet for your sake He became poor, so that you by His poverty might become rich. Paul's first argument is Christological. The "grace" of Christ is in His act of self-sacrifice for the benefit of us. It is forever amazing that though this text is Paul's chief Christological argument for charity, the text is rarely used in that fashion today. Paul uses the great "happy exchange" (Luther) of the rich/poor metaphor for obvious reasons in motivating the Corinthians to charitable giving. "Have this mind among yourselves . . . though He was in the form of God . . . [He] emptied Himself, by taking the form of a servant" (Philippians 2:5–7). Paul had already introduced the langue of "exchange" in 1 Corinthians 1:18: "The cross is folly to those who are perishing, but to us . . . it is the power of God."

The Second Proof

¹⁰And in this matter I give my judgment: this benefits you, who a year ago started not only to do this work but also to desire to do it. Paul refers to a matter of common sense (judgment/*gnomen*).[76] "You started this thing, it makes sense to finish, doesn't it?" "You are the one who wanted to do it a year ago. Wouldn't it be a good thing now for you to finish it?" Paul appeals to basic human common sense. Within that year, much had taken place, including Paul's strong rebuke of the Corinthians for a number of delicate problems. Paul is saying, "Let's overlook all that and get it done."

¹¹So now finish doing it as well, so that your readiness in desiring it may be matched by your completing it out of what you have. The Corinthians began the collection out of sincere desire. The desire grew cold because

---

76   Betz, *2 Corinthians*, 63.

of the numerous problems in the congregation. Paul's great pastoral sense is that they will benefit in every way by focusing on external needs rather than only on those internal to the congregation. The apostle urges the completion of the task on a reasonable basis, that is, out of what they have (*ek tou exein*).

[12]*For if the readiness is there, it is acceptable according to what a person has, not according to what he does not have.* "Readiness" (*prothumia*) indicates eagerness. Thus the Bereans eagerly investigated the Scriptures (*meta pases prothumias*; Acts 17:11). Paul is concerned with honest and sincere motives, not with the amount of money.

DISCUSSION QUESTIONS 10

The congregation in Corinth suffered many divisions and conflicts. Describe some of the conflicts your congregation has faced in recent years.

_____

_____

How might focusing on an external need in another congregation or another part of the world help a congregation heal and move on?

_____

_____

The Third Proof

[13]*I do not mean that others should be eased and you burdened, but that as a matter of fairness.* Paul's final proof appeals to the Corinthians' sense of equity or fairness.[77] Paul did not have "ease" or "rest" (*anesis*) for his spirit when he could not find Titus in Troas (2 Corinthians 2:13). *Thlipsis* (here rendered "burdened") indicates affliction, material/financial need. "Fairness" (*isotetos*) is often rendered incorrectly as "equality." Paul urges:

---

77   Betz, *2 Corinthians*, 67.

"Masters, treat your bondservants justly and fairly (*isotata*), knowing that you also have a Master in heaven" (Colossians 4:1). The virtue indicates reasonable care for all.

[14]*your abundance at the present time should supply their need, so that their abundance may supply your need, that there may be fairness.* "Need" (*hysterema*) means a lack of any sort ("fall short of the glory of God" [Romans 3:23]; "not lacking in any gift" [1 Corinthians 1:7]). "Fairness" is a good rendering again of *isotes* rather than "equality." Paul here indicates that while the Corinthians supply the physical needs of those in Jerusalem, the latter have supplied their spiritual needs. Jesus said, "For salvation is from the Jews" (John 4:22; Romans 11:11–36).

[15]*As it is written, "Whoever gathered much had nothing left over, and whoever gathered little had no lack."* Paul evidently cites from memory—the word order in the Septuagint being slightly different. The apostle probably conflates the Hebrew original with the Greek, being familiar with both. "They gathered, some more, some less. But when they measured it with an omer, whoever gathered much had nothing left over, and whoever gathered little had no lack. Each of them gathered as much as he could eat" (Exodus 16:17–18). When the Old Testament people of God gathered the manna that fell, they did not all gather equal amounts (due to age, ability, etc.), yet all ate. So in the church all are cared for by sharing the provisions God supplies. It is significant that Paul applies this text speaking of all the Old Testament people who were in one locale to the church strewn from Palestine to Greece! It is also significant that Paul applies a text speaking of the special and specific prerogative of the Jews ("our fathers ate manna") to the entire "mixed" church of Jew and Gentile believers (Oschwald).

8:16–23 The Legal Section
(Commendation and Authorization of the Envoys)

The Commendation of Titus

[16]*But thanks be to God, who put into the heart of Titus the same earnest care I have for you.* Betz notes that here Paul switches from arguments

to official business.[78] "Earnest care" (*spoudeis*) is repeatedly used in these chapters for eager active desire. It is God's gift resulting from belief in the Gospel. Titus shares the apostle's concerns and ministry in every way (see above). Betz notes the use of *spoude* in secular literature of administration. For the administrator of such a collection, there was no more important quality to have.[79]

[17]*For he not only accepted our appeal, but being himself very earnest he is going to you of his own accord.* Titus accepted Paul's appeal (*paraklesis*; "exhortation"). Betz has an intriguing excursus on the commissioning of Titus and the brothers as a formal mandatum or officium/office. The word *paraklesis* is common to such contracts in Greek society of the day. Titus was given a legal mandate to carry out tasks on behalf of Paul. By Roman law, when a citizen in good standing accepted such a public obligation, that obligation was to be fulfilled without any financial compensation.[80] Such a mandate described the agent's personality, qualifications, and standing in the community and the specific assignment. The importance of the matter and the large sum of money involved required just such a mandate according to Betz, from Paul to Titus and the brothers. Paul dealt with his compatriots in the same manner as the Corinthians regarding requests. Nothing out of compulsion but rather out of conviction. So Titus willingly was most eager to come to the Corinthians to take care of the matter of the collection. Being with Paul from the days at Antioch and the visit to Jerusalem, the matter was of personal significance to him. So he, too, comes "of his own accord" (*authairetos*) being very zealous (*spoudaioteros*).

The Commendation of the Two Brothers

[18]*With him we are sending the brother who is famous among all the churches for his preaching of the gospel.* We simply have no idea who this brother was. There is no textual evidence that the name was removed (because he allegedly later fell out of the good graces of Paul or the church). Some

---

78   Betz, *2 Corinthians*, 70.
79   Betz, *2 Corinthians*, 70.
80   Betz, *2 Corinthians*, 71.

have suggested Luke was one of them (Plummer).[81] In any case, this man had a stellar reputation.

[19]*And not only that, but he has been appointed by the churches to travel with us as we carry out this act of grace that is being ministered by us, for the glory of the Lord Himself and to show our good will.* "Appointed" (*xeirotoneo*) means "extending the hand." Thus the brother was elected by the churches for the task of working with Paul in carrying out the collection. Paul left Titus in Crete to appoint (*katastasei*) elders (Titus 1). In Acts 14, Paul and Barnabas "appointed" (*xeirotoneo*) elders for them in every church" (Acts 14:23). Yet these appointments all probably occurred as did the choosing of the seven in Acts 6. The community put forward ("elected"; *exelexanto*) the seven names, and the apostles appointed (*katastesomen*) them (6:4–5). So also Paul indicated that those "accredit[ed] by letter" by the Corinthians would accompany him to Jerusalem with the collection (1 Corinthians 16:3). There is no pitting of apostle against people or vice versa.

[20]*We take this course so that no one should blame us about this generous gift that is being administered by us.* Thus Paul would not want the delegates for the collection to merely be his own choice! "Administered" renders the verbal form of *diakonia*, which for Paul had become a technical term for matters of the collection. The apostle wanted in every way to avoid suspicion. The Roman world was filled with unscrupulous frauds who raised collections for worthy causes, but then kept the money for themselves.[82] In calling the gift "generous" (*hadrotes*), Paul indicates that the gift was to be very substantial.[83]

[21]*for we aim at what is honorable not only in the Lord's sight but also in the sight of man.* Paul loosely quotes Proverbs 3:4: "So you will find favor and good success in the sight of God and man." He makes a similar statement in Romans 12:17: "Give thought to what is honorable in the sight of all." Thus one is to aim not only for honorable motives (known to God) but the appearance of honor over against men. The brothers would ensure that honor. Given the deep challenges Paul faced particularly in Asia

---

81   Betz, *2 Corinthians*, 73.

82   Betz, *2 Corinthians*, 76.

83   Meeks, *The First Urban Christians*, 65.

(Ephesus), it is understandable that he is so adamant on both the reality and appearance of honor with respect to the collection.

22And with them we are sending our brother whom we have often tested and found earnest in many matters, but who is now more earnest than ever because of his great confidence in you. Another man is added who is more "earnest" than ever—that is, both eager and capable (*spoudaion*). Who is he? We have no idea. He's called "our" brother by Paul, and this may indicate a closer association with the apostle. Perhaps he was, in fact, appointed by Paul. The Acts 20 list indicated that each church probably had two delegates to Jerusalem. Why does Paul name a third? He already had appointed Titus. Betz surmises that perhaps the "brother" chosen by the Corinthians necessitated a third be insisted upon by Paul! Thus the delegation from Corinth would include (1) Titus (Paul's man); (2) the brother chosen by Corinth; and (3) another man chosen by Paul and also appointed by the churches.[84]

The Authorization of the Delegates

23As for Titus, he is my partner and fellow worker for your benefit. And as for our brothers, they are messengers of the churches, the glory of Christ. This is the legal language of appointment. Paul is making it clear that he has authorized Titus to be his legal representative to administer the collection in Corinth.[85] Paul calls Titus his "partner" (*koinonos*) and "fellow worker" (*synergos*), indicating the nature of Titus's authority, which was nearly that of the apostle by virtue of his association. The word "messengers" translates "apostles" (*apostoloi*), taken here in the sense of those sent with a commission by the churches themselves as official representatives. Thus Paul was an "apostle of Christ," or Christ's ambassador, carrying the full authority of Christ Himself.

---

84   Betz, *2 Corinthians*, 78.
85   Betz, *2 Corinthians*, 79.

DISCUSSION QUESTIONS 11

Why was it wise for Paul to have each congregation select its own delegates instead of appointing them himself?

_____

_____

Why is it important to establish the credentials of any organization or cause to which a congregation contributes?

_____

_____

8:24 The Peroratio
(Peroration—Summary and Final Statement of Purpose)

²⁴*So give proof before the churches of your love and of our boasting about you to these men.* What's the point of all that preceded? It's time to bring the collection to fruition and, in doing so, not make Paul out to be a liar.

9:1–2 The Exordium
(Introduction)

9:1 *Now it is superfluous for me to write to you about the ministry for the saints.* "Now concerning the collection (*diakonias*)." Paul turns from the technical language of properly and legally appointed delegates back to the matter at hand. "It is superfluous" because he knows they know why he is writing and much of what he will say.

²*for I know your readiness, of which I boast about you to the people of Macedonia, saying that Achaia has been ready since last year. And your zeal has stirred up most of them.* Apparently, Titus, when he came to Paul reporting the sad state of affairs in Corinth with respect to the collection, told the apostle things with Achaia in general were much better. So Paul had boasted of the work of the Achaians to the Macedonians. That spurred on

the Macedonians. Paul, in turn, used the results among the Macedonians to cajole the Corinthians![86]

9:3–5a The Narratio
(Statement of Facts)

[3]*But I am sending the brothers so that our boasting about you may not prove empty (vain) in this matter, so that you may be ready, as I said you would be.* The brothers (capable administrators) would assist the Corinthians so Paul's boasting would not prove an embarrassment to him or the Corinthians. "Vain" (*kenow*; render void/empty). "I would rather die than have anyone deprive me of my ground for boasting" (1 Corinthians 9:15).

[4]*Otherwise, if some Macedonians come with me and find that you are not ready, we would be humiliated—to say nothing of you—for being so confident.* Would the Macedonian delegates already accompany Paul? Apparently so. Paul desires to bring them along to assist with the Corinthian collection. He'll have three months to pull it together before taking the full delegation to Jerusalem (Acts 20:1–2). "Some Macedonians" might have included Sopater of Berea or Aristarchus and Secundus of Thessalonica (Acts 20:4).

[5]*So I thought it necessary to urge the brothers to go on ahead to you.* Paul had to finish the work in Macedonia and thought it best to send the brothers rather than cut his time short in the north to come south and tend to the Corinthian challenge.

9:5b The Propositio
(Proposition—What Now Needs to Be Done)

and arrange in advance for the gift you have promised. The advance team hit the ground in Corinth no doubt carrying 2 Corinthians itself. *so that it may be ready as a willing gift, not as an exaction.* Paul now turns from past to future.[87] Paul wants a "blessing" (*eulogia*), not something forced out of them (*pleonexia*). *Eulogia* is a blessing wrought by grace, willingly bestowed. "Blessed be the God and Father of our Lord Jesus Christ, who has blessed (*eulogesas*) us in Christ with every spiritual blessing (*eulogia*

86 Betz, *2 Corinthians*, 93.
87 Betz, *2 Corinthians*, 95.

pneumatike)" (Ephesians 1:3). "What do you have that you did not receive?" (1 Corinthians 4:7). "Exaction" translates "greed" (*pleonexia*). "Take care, and be on your guard against all covetousness (*pleonexia*), for one's life does not consist in the abundance of his possessions" (Luke 12:15). *Pleonexia* is frequent in Paul's catalogs of the sins of unbelief (Romans 1:29; Ephesians 5:3; Colossians 3:5). Here Paul's concern is that he not be accused of greed for urging the completion of the collection, in the sense of "For we never came with words of flattery, as you know, nor with a pretext for greed—God is witness" (1 Thessalonians 2:5).

9:6–14 The Probatio
(Proofs—The Proofs Justify the Author's Concerns)[88]

The Thesis

⁶*The point is this: whoever sows sparingly will also reap sparingly, and whoever sows bountifully will also reap bountifully.* This proverb echoes the thought of Proverbs 11:24, though with no similarity in wording: "One gives freely, yet grows all the richer; another withholds what he should give, and only suffers want." Paul uses the word *spare* of the supreme gift: "He who did not spare (*pheidomai*) His own Son but gave Him up for us all, how will He not also with Him graciously give us all things?" (Romans 8:32). The simple but profound truth is that if the farmer skimps on seed, the harvest will be poor. Paul had used the agricultural metaphor in 1 Corinthians 15 for the resurrection. "It is sown in dishonor; it is raised in glory" (1 Corinthians 15:43), and then he proceeded directly to discuss the collection (1 Corinthians 16). The Lord Himself did not spare His own Son, and the harvest was phenomenal. The text is exceedingly memorable and more so in the original, "sparingly, sparingly" . . . "upon blessings, upon blessings." If one sows "upon blessings" ("*eulogiais*" in light of blessings received from God), one shall harvest "upon blessings." That is to say, the blessings will be heaped up. The divine economy of life is counterintuitive. The following verses explicate the "gift of blessing."

---

88 Betz, *2 Corinthians*, 100.

The First Proof—the Giver

⁷Each one must give as he has decided in his heart, not reluctantly or under compulsion, for God loves a cheerful giver. Literally, "each as he has decided ahead of time in his heart." So, giving is always a matter of the heart, but Paul wants the matter to be deliberative and rational, in light of blessings received. Not "reluctantly" (*ek lupes*). "Godly grief (*lupe*) produces a repentance" (2 Corinthians 7:10). The opposite is grief according to greed. The decision to give is to be a deliberative resolution, which considers one's blessings and avoids "reluctance." The Gospel broaches no "compulsion" (*anagkes*). "I preferred to do nothing without your consent in order that your goodness might not be by compulsion but of your own accord" (Philemon 14). Paul recognized that people can provide gifts for a number of reasons. Some can result from internal distress, others from external pressure. God was looking for gifts that came freely as a loving, grateful response to God's love.[89] Proverbs 8 (Septuagint) states, "God blesses (*eulogei*) a man who is a cheerful giver."

The Second Proof

⁸And God is able to make all grace abound to you, so that having all sufficiency in all things at all times, you may abound in every good work. God is the actor. He makes a "cheerful giver." How? "He gives overflowing grace (*charis*) so that in all things, all times, with all sufficiency (*panti, pantote, pasan*) you may abound in every (*pan*) good work." The grace of God causes the recognition that in all things we are blessed. Grace produces abundance—not in a "name it and claim it" sort of theology of glory, but rather a sober and joyous recognition that God's provision suffices for need and abounds for others' needs. Grace piles up blessings—"all grace," "all sufficiency," "all things," "all times," "every good work." There is no cause to be stingy.

> *⁹As it is written,*
> *"He has distributed freely, he has given to the poor;*
> *his righteousness endures forever."*

---

89 Betz, *2 Corinthians*, 105.

Paul imports teaching from a psalm that is meaningful for his work of the collection.

Praise the LORD!
Blessed is the man who fears the LORD,
who greatly delights in His commandments!
His offspring will be mighty in the land;
the generation of the upright will be blessed.
Wealth and riches are in his house,
and his righteousness endures forever.
Light dawns in the darkness for the upright;
he is gracious, merciful, and righteous.
It is well with the man who deals generously and lends;
who conducts his affairs with justice. . . .
He has distributed freely;
he has given to the poor;
his righteousness endures forever;
his horn is exalted in honor.
The wicked man sees it and is angry;
he gnashes his teeth and melts away;
the desire of the wicked will perish!
(Psalm 112:1–5, 9–10, emphasis added)

[10]*He who supplies seed to the sower and bread for food will supply and multiply your seed for sowing and increase the harvest of your righteousness.* God provides the seed for sowing and bread for eating. The Corinthians' charity is promised a divine blessing to multiply their harvest in the future. Give, and you shall be blessed with all the more. "The harvest of your righteousness" is the harvest produced by the righteousness of Christ.

[11]*You will be enriched in every way to be generous in every way, which through us will produce thanksgiving to God.* Another promise of sweeping divine blessing: "every way" (*en panti*) you will be made rich "for all generosity" (*pasan aploteta*). The promise is that the Corinthians will be made wealthy in every possible way, materially and spiritually. In this sense, wealth is a wonderful gift of God, seeing that it gives the opportunity for

believers to show generosity to God's people in need.[90] Through Paul's delivery of the gift, there will result "thanksgiving" (*eucharistia*) to God on the part of the poor in Jerusalem. Paul encourages giving by telling the Corinthians that their giving will result in divine transactions.

DISCUSSION QUESTIONS 12

Why is it important that offerings and collections be given freely from the heart and not by compulsion or from selfish motivation?

_____

_____

_____

What should a Christian do if he or she is reluctant to make a contribution?

_____

_____

_____

Is there ever a time when a person should not make a contribution?

_____

_____

_____

The Fourth Proof

[12]*For the ministry of this service is not only supplying the needs of the saints, but is also overflowing in many thanksgivings to God.* "The *diakonia* of this *leitourgia*." *Diakonia* is Paul's technical term for the collection, "charitable service." A *leitourgia* is when private citizens choose to do a public service without compensation of any form.[91] The need addressed among the saints is worthy in and of itself, but the gift will also be a great

---

90 Betz, *2 Corinthians,* 115.
91 Betz, *2 Corinthians,* 117.

aid to their faith and result in abundant thanksgiving. Thus the giving has a physical and a spiritual purpose.

The Fifth Proof

[13]*By their approval of this service, they will glorify God because of your submission that comes from your confession of the gospel of Christ, and the generosity of your contribution for them and for all others.* "By their confirmation (*dokimes*) of the *diakonia*"—that is, knowing exactly from whom it comes and why it was given—they will glorify God. Why has it come? It is a submission produced by the Corinthians' confession (*homologias*) of the Gospel. The very gift is itself a confession of the Gospel. "Contribution" is *koinonias*, a "sharing" or "fellowship." So "fellowship" in the church is not merely doctrinal assent. It is mutual participation in Christ's gifts of Word and Sacrament and also sharing in the goods and material challenges of life.[92]

[14]*while they long for you and pray for you, because of the surpassing grace of God upon you.* An added benefit of the gift is that the poor in Jerusalem will pray for the Corinthians and "drink deep" for you. So Paul can say to his co-workers, "I long—drink deep—to see you." A great blessing considering the deep animus on the part of zealotic Christians over against Gentiles!

9:15 The Peroratio
(Peroration)

[15]*Thanks be to God for His inexpressible gift!* Here Paul places the great collection in its proper perspective. This act of love was prompted and surpassed by God's grace in giving His Son for the salvation of all people. Our gifts to one another flow from that greatest gift as a notion of thanksgiving to God.[93]

---

92 For Paul knew precisely that the refusal of the gifts of the other congregations by the Church in Jerusalem would indicate the breaking of the unity of the church. The sacrifice, whose collection he organized everywhere, had for Paul a very eminent theological significance. That's why he spoke of it so often. It is decisive that this collection was designated as "fellowship." Thus it appears to me that the ecumenical collection of the apostle not only replaced the Jewish temple tax, but rather at the same time lengthened and continued the fellowship of goods worked by the Holy Ghost in Jerusalem [i.e., Acts 3–6]. Oscar Cullmann, "Ökumenische Kollekte und Gütergemeinschaft im Urchristentum," 600–604, in Vorträge und Aufsätze 1925–1962. (Mohr/Siebeck, Tübingen 1966), 602. My translation.

93 Dunn, *The Theology of Paul*, 707.

SO WHAT?

The collection was Paul's crowning achievement in life. It is fairly amazing that this great Christian theologian and missionary so decisively and determinedly turned his attention to a matter of human need. And he led the entire Gentile mission to take up the matter of human need as a corporate, churchly act. He saw in this need the deepest theological significance. The most tangible demonstration of unity and love in the church—aside from the Word and Sacraments, which constitute such love—is the sharing of one's possessions with the needy in the Body of Christ. "Fellowship" is, for Paul, participation in Christ and by extension mutual participation in one another. The church is a fellowship (*koinonia*). The collection is so much a demonstration, a tangible evidence of the fellowship, that Paul dares to call it a *koinonia*. What do we learn from the collection?

1. Grace (divine favor) produces grace (gracious living).

2. Church fellowship includes concern for physical needs.

3. Paul and his ordained apostolic band were concerned with both physical and spiritual need and worked extensively to both ends.

4. *Diakonia* may well be a powerful tool for enhancing and maintaining church unity. It produces prayer and thanksgiving to God for the giver.

5. Giving is a demonstration of confession of the Gospel.

6. The church is to demonstrate the utmost care in all matters financial.

7. The church does well to follow Paul's careful methods of accountability, administration, and transparency, with direct local representation.

8. Appointment to offices of responsibility ought to be shared by local communities affected.

9. Meeting human need is the most basic reason for Christian stewardship.

10. Giving is in no way to be done out of compulsion or with a bad conscience.

11. Giving is best done after careful deliberation and consideration of blessings.

12. God is pleased with each gift (small or large) relative to the faith, intent, and means of the giver.

13. Spiritual care and counsel for the giver was worthy of the deepest apostolic concern. It also ought to concern our clergy. Giving is a deeply theological and pastoral concern.[94]

14. It is very appropriate to reference, as did Paul, the promises of Holy Scripture with respect to generosity in encouraging giving.

15. Giving to the needy carries the New Testament promise of abundant blessing (not withstanding the theology of the cross, of course).

16. Based on the model of St. Paul, the church would do well to have competent, theologically capable men or women administering funding issues.

17. Mission congregations must not be spared the privilege of learning to give to those in need outside their immediate community, no matter how modest the gift.

---

94 Dunn discusses how Paul was very sensitive to the feelings and views of the Gentiles from whom he gathered the collections for the benefit of the Jews. In every way, Paul wanted to walk alongside the contributing congregations rather than force them to do something they didn't first want to do. This gives us a glimpse into more than Paul's leadership and pastoral cares; it shows us his very heart. See Dunn, The Theology of Paul, 710:

DISCUSSION QUESTIONS 13

Why was Paul martyred?

_____

_____

_____

Looking through this list of seventeen "lessons," which strike you
as most important for your congregation when considering assisting
other Christians in need?

_____

_____

_____

How does this entire list help keep a congregation grounded in its
purpose for existing in the world?

_____

_____

_____

LEADER GUIDE

DISCUSSION QUESTIONS 1

Describe a disaster that impacted you or someone you know. What kinds of relief were needed? Who provided them?

[Leader: These could be disasters that struck your local area or were experienced in other places by members of your group. The goal is to recognize how crucial relief efforts are in such times. It also gets the group brainstorming different ways to respond to disasters, including those happening in other parts of the country.]

Why might a Christian community choose to direct their aid to Christian brothers and sisters in need rather than to all the victims, believers and unbelievers alike?

[Leader: When Christian victims are assisted and their immediate needs met, they are freed up to love and serve their neighbors—perhaps by sharing some of the relief gifts they received. This is in fact exactly what the congregation-based disaster work of LCMS World Relief and Human Care does.]

What benefits come out of the whole congregation or community joining together in a collection rather than just a few interested individuals?

[Leader: Increasing the ownership of such collections unites a congregation or group of congregations. It expands the community's awareness outside of its own needs and interests. It unites the larger Body of Christ and provides opportunities to share the Gospel with unbelievers affected.]

DISCUSSION QUESTIONS 2

The apostles appointed the seven in Acts 6:1–6 to oversee the distribution of contributions among the Christians in Jerusalem. Why is it significant that Paul stayed with one of these seven on his way to Jerusalem?

[Leader: If Paul is bringing a gift for the Jews in Jerusalem, it is likely some of these seven will have a part in overseeing the distribution of this collection as well.]

If your congregation or a group of neighboring congregations was raising a collection for the congregations in an area of need, what value would you expect to find in communicating with the disaster response arm of LCMS World Relief and Human Care?

[Leader: LCMS World Relief and Human Care is working with the receiving congregations to better assess what objects/gifts are needed and how best to deliver them. In fact, many send material things that they perceive as needed or appreciated by disaster victims but are not. LCMS World Relief and Human Care sends only what congregations and districts request.]

DISCUSSION QUESTIONS 3

Name some of the issues that divide congregations today.

[Leader: Educational levels, socioeconomic status, musical and liturgical differences, models of church governance, and so forth.]

How have you seen such divisions hamper a congregation's ministry?

[Leader: Answers will vary. But it is usually easy to spot a selfish, sinful motivation fueling the division and draining off the congregation's energy and effective witness.

DISCUSSION QUESTIONS 4

How can a congregation benefit from collecting gifts that will leave the area and be sent to other Christians far away?

[Leader: Members are reminded that we are all part of the one Body of Christ, the mystical Body known as the Church. We will spend eternity together in the glory of God, so we can assist one another today.]

Recipients of our collections clearly benefit in material ways. How do they also benefit spiritually or theologically?

[Leader: The chief spiritual benefits are recognizing God's providence through their brother and sister Christians and the kindling of their love for fellow Christian brothers and sisters.]

DISCUSSION QUESTIONS 5

Reread Paul's comments about Titus in 2 Corinthians 7:5–9. What does this show us about the important role Titus played in Paul's ministry?

[Leader: Not only did Titus do important ministerial oversight on Paul's behalf, but he also comforted and greatly encouraged Paul and his team when they struggled with external troubles and inner fears in Macedonia.]

What are some ways you become a greater source of comfort and encouragement to your pastor?

[Leader: Often, pastors are supported by a majority of members in a congregation, but those members remain silent. Frequently, a pastor hears only the voices of those who disapprove or want to stir up problems. You can encourage your pastor through your kind and reassuring words and defend him to members who needlessly harass him.]

DISCUSSION QUESTIONS 6

What impact would it make on the struggling Jewish Christians in Jerusalem to see so many Gentile delegates bringing the large relief offering from those other regions?

[Leader: Paul knew there were tensions between the Jewish and Gentile Christians. This huge delegation would impress on the Jewish Christians how Christ had built His Church among the Gentiles and encourage them to accept and embrace their Gentile brothers and sisters who eagerly wanted to help their Judean brothers and sisters.]

How is this similar to huge, synodwide collections?

[Leader: The needy recipients see the love of their Christian brothers and sisters—and from pooling together gifts from so many congregations, the offerings are sizable and able to make a huge impact.]

DISCUSSION QUESTIONS 7

Describe a time you did something for someone with the best of intentions but were met with skepticism and condemnation.

[Leader: We want to explore the natural reaction to such treatment—the bitterness and resentment that tempts us never to be so generous again.]

What are some things you can do to avoid bitterness and resentment when your generosity is sorely mistreated?

[Leader: Prayer is always important, especially as we remember how Jesus' generosity and love was rewarded with persecution, torture, and death. Yet, Jesus prayed, "Father, forgive them," and He realized they did not know what they were doing. We can pray that God would open their eyes, and we can take consolation in the fact that God knows the truth of our generosity. We can also focus on those who are truly grateful for the things we do.]

DISCUSSION QUESTIONS 8

What opportunities can disaster relief provide for Christian mission-aries and relief agencies in areas where overt witness is illegal?

[Leader: Although it is often delicate working to aid people where an overt witness is illegal, aid leads to contacts, quiet sharing of the Gospel, and opportunities to build relationships.]

DISCUSSION QUESTIONS 9

How is the Macedonians' generosity reminiscent of the poor widow who put all she had in the offering box at the temple (Mark 12:42–43)?

[Leader: The widow showed complete trust in God by giving away all the money she had to take care of herself. Likewise, the Macedonians couldn't really afford it, but they trusted God's providence for them and insisted on taking part in the collection for Jerusalem. Perhaps they realized there were people suffering even worse poverty than they were.]

How do you balance generosity in offerings (and demonstrating that faith to your family) with being responsible with your family's finances?

[Leader: This is a balance every family must strike—faith and trust that God will provide with wise stewardship of the gifts God gives. Some families will sacrifice a luxury they would have enjoyed and contribute that instead as an offering.]

DISCUSSION QUESTIONS 10

The congregation in Corinth suffered many divisions and conflicts. Describe some of the conflicts your congregation has faced in recent years.

[Leader: These could be differences of opinion that threaten to divide a congregation or afflictions that tempt people to give up.]

How might focusing on an external need in another congregation or another part of the world help a congregation heal and move on?

[Leader: It often helps us to find someone suffering worse than we are. That draws us back to God and one another with thankful hearts and minds.]

DISCUSSION QUESTIONS 11

Why was it wise for Paul to have each congregation select its own delegates instead of appointing them himself?

[Leader: Paul wanted to give the congregations every confidence that their collection was actually going to the poor in Jerusalem, just as the collection had been described to them.]

Why is it important to establish the credentials of any organization or cause to which a congregation contributes?

[Leader: These gifts are given out of faith and gratitude by the members of the congregation. They have had the power to call their pastor and elect officers who would oversee this collection, but they need to be assured that the gifts will be used wisely at the other end, where they are received.]

DISCUSSION QUESTIONS 12

Why is it important that offerings and collections be given freely from the heart and not by compulsion or from selfish motivation?

[Leader: God gave His Son to save us willingly and freely, and Jesus offered Himself voluntarily. The Gospel and our response to it must come from faith, love, and gratitude, never from selfish ambition or reluctant compulsion.]

What should a Christian do if he or she is reluctant to make a contribution?

[Leader: This calls for self-examination. Does the reluctance arise from fear that the giver will not have enough once this gift is given? That calls for repentance and greater trust in God by studying God's faithfulness. Does it arise out of selfish greed masquerading as concern for family finances? That calls for repentance and prayer. Is it born out of distrust of whoever is promoting the collection? It is never wrong to ask more questions and seek clarification.]

Is there ever a time when a person should not make a contribution?

[Leader: Perhaps if a person feels forced, or coerced, or if he or she has planned charitable giving and desires to execute those plans. Giving is also done in light of the primary vocations an individual has as a parent, child, congregation member, and so on. Note the apostle says the gift "is acceptable according to what a person has, not according to what he does not have" (2 Corinthians 8:12). Our actions, including giving, will always be clouded by sin. But we can always give, knowing our sins, including greed and wrong motivation, are forgiven.]

DISCUSSION QUESTIONS 13

Why was Paul martyred?

[Leader: The obvious answer is that Paul was put to death for preaching the Gospel. But notice that Paul was arrested in Acts 21:27–35 while delivering the collection to Jerusalem. He was then forced to appeal to Caesar because of Jewish plots to kill him if he was returned to Jerusalem for trial as Festus intended (Acts 25:3–5).]

Looking through this list of seventeen "lessons," which strike you as most important for your congregation when considering assisting other Christians in need?

[Leader: Answers will vary, but consider how they might reflect on a previous fundraising activity in the church that could have gone better.]

How does this entire list help keep a congregation grounded in its purpose for existing in the world?

[God formed the Church to make disciples, much like Jesus did in His ministry. When He saw physical need, He met it by healing the sick and feeding the hungry. He showed His concern for people by caring for the needs of body and soul. Sometimes, He cared for physical needs that led to care for spiritual needs. Christian congregations likewise will demonstrate concern for spiritual and physical needs.]

NOTES